F

"Marriage is not only be navigated with the help of God. The process of becoming one is not a single event but a journey we navigate through seasons of good and bad. I believe God gives us grace for the assignment of marriage and it is by "grace we are saved" which tells me this gift can be applied to our daily lives and relationships. Carlette and Chris were trusted by God with trouble. This book will reveal to the reader that this trust was not wasted but trouble was utilized as a tool to propel them into purpose. Their testimony is like a transparent oil that is poured out and the reader will be the benefit of its fragrance. These are not just empty words on a page, but it's is their raw and unfiltered truth and they have dared to share it with you no matter the risk. The Bible tells us the truth will make us free. It is my desire that as you the reader digest these pages that you too will experience the freedom of the truth of your situation whatever it may be. It is only then that God came come in a heal that which is broken. You will be challenged yet changed knowing that when "life interruptions" occur God doesn't expect you to be perfect, He wants to perfect you as you seek Him every step of the way! It's is only then you will see the "beauty" in the "battle."

—**Pastor Danielle Murphy**
The dReam Center Church of Atlanta

"Inopportune disruptions appear to be hindrances to our well laid plans; although frustrating, we must embrace them as opportunities to participate with God in His plans for our lives. Chris and Carlette are evidence that whether insignificant or monumental, when our lives are altered by brief diversions our response must be one of faith.

Individually and collectively, both Chris and Carlette demonstrate love for God, His word, and His service. Cancer is no small matter; rather than blame God, they chose to see God.

They further show how marriage can become strained under the weight of interruptions. They made note of all they learned and share those same action steps at the end of this book. Each step will charge each partner to deny themselves for the greater good of their relationship.

From start to finish, the transparency and authenticity in this book will fill your heart with joy as you read their beautiful beginnings and endow you with empowerment to face life's challenges with unrelenting faith."

—Daren and Nakia Blakely

"There is one theme that stood out among all the other information that Chris and Carlette presents in this book and that is the power of prayer. This is a must read for everyone navigating through life's storms or in preparation for one. The Bible tells us that man must always pray and not faint. (Luke 18:1)

This book is a refreshing reminder that prayer is the vehicle that ignites our destinies. As we adapt to life's transitions, God gets glory out of every situation in our lives when we surrender to Him. Chris and Carlette's testimony teach us that prayer fortifies us in the midst of life's most turbulent interruptions."

—V. Terrill Hill

Life's Interruptions

Life's Interruptions

"When my wife was diagnosed with cancer, I didn't know where to turn. This book is for men who are chosen to walk beside their wives in battle."
—E. Chris Edwards

E. CHRIS & CARLETTE EDWARDS

Life's Interruptions by E. Chris & Carlette Edwards
©2021

Unless otherwise noted all Scripture quotations are from the King James Version of the Bible.

Scripture quotations marked NLT are from the Holy Bible, New Living Translation, copyright © 1996,2004, 2007. Used by permission of Tyndale House Publishers, Inc., Wheaton, IL 60189. All rights reserved.

Scripture quotations marked NKJV are from the New King James Version of the Bible. Copyright ©1979, 1980, 1982 by Thomas Nelson, Inc., publishers. Used by permission.

Printed in the United States of America.

Edwards Media Group LLC
www.lifeinterruptions.com

Photographer: Anthony Dallas
Cover Design: Ferland Antwine
Interior Design: Marvin D. Cloud

DEDICATION

This book is dedicated to our friend Dr. Okechi Nwabara, the man who pushed us to explore the pain in my breast. We are certain that our visit was necessary and vital to God's miraculous plan.

ACKNOWLEDGMENTS

Chris

Carlette and I are grateful and humbled by the experiences that shaped and molded us.

"Consider it pure joy, my brothers and sisters, whenever you face trials of many kinds, because you know that the testing of your faith produces perseverance. Let perseverance finish its work so that you may be mature and complete, not lacking anything" (James 1:2-4).

Thank you, Lord, for doing what you do best. You strengthened our marriage and brought us closer together as husband and wife.

I thank my parents, Elmer and Imogene, who groomed me to be a loving husband. Dad, you worked hard to make sure that (we) your family were always taken care of. Your kind and caring nature was instilled within me. Mom, you also worked hard to be sure we didn't lack anything. As of 2021, you guys are still kicking, and your union of 67 years serves as a portrait of possibility for a lasting marriage. You model the strength and love it takes for couples to know that marriage can last through the good, the bad, and the indifferent.

Thank you, my big sister, Joi, for always being there and concerned about Carlette and I. As you have faced a similar trial, know that God has your back and He has also brought you through.

To my friend, who is now singing and dancing with the Lord and the angels, Eddie Taylor. I think of you a lot. If it were not for you, my faith and spiritual path would not have gone this way. Your consistent concern for me allowed God to shape me in His image. Thank you so much!

My boy, Reggie Lillie; you may not know the impact you had in my life during this time, but I appreciate the times you listened to me and allowed me to vent.

Daren, not only did you come check me out before Carlette came out to the car on our first date, but you always gave sound advice.

Carlette, thank you for not getting too upset with me. This was a trying time in our marriage, but we made it through. It seemed like an eternity while we were going through this battle but looking back, it feels like it was a short moment in time. Love you, baby!

Carlette

In this experience, I really saw the handiwork and sovereignty of God. My knowledge of Christ and His finished work expanded. I pray that you learn through our testimony, the weight [magnitude, potency, and power] of the words we speak. God's Word is true and powerful, and there is nothing like taking Him at His Word and trusting that same power to be displayed in and through us. My Father, I am forever grateful…I literally could not make it without you.

Thank you to my family:

To my parents, Reverend Dewitt and Lady Sharon L. Jackson; my Eldest brother and my sister in love, Reverend Javaughn and Lady Felicia B. Blakely; my youngest brother and sister in love, Mr. Dewitt Jr. and Alisa Jackson. And to my host of cousins, particularly Reverend Gary and Sandra Bush; and Ms. Willette O. Blakely. You all travelled the highways for appointments, surgery, and recovery. Thank you for your dedication.

To the Rock Community Church pastors and family; it was great to go through this process and have a praying church with a house of authentic worship. Your steadfastness and acts of kindness were needed and appreciated. You kept me focused and for that I'm grateful.

There were many people in the faith community who were by my side every step of the way, not just in word, but also in deed. Particularly Pastor Harry and Lady Etiwanda Beard and the City of Refuge COGIC family. You called and sent fresh fruit and food. Lady Etiwanda had a call schedule for my treatment days, and most of all, Pastor Harry Beard had his entire church congregation go on a fast and *all-night* prayer shut-in at their church, just for "me" all the way in Kokomo, Indiana.

To the Beard family; you know our families have strong ties. And the Blakely family; thank you for being committed to the bond and taking care of me naturally and spiritually.

Pastor Denise Carpenter, thank you for being a shoulder to cry on, and a prayer partner. You kept the Word of God before me and remained an extreme encourager. As my nutritionist (you made me carry around blueberries and almonds) and finally you showed me how to be glamorous and fabulous while going through breast cancer treatment. Thank you for introducing me to Ms. Cookie, the master hairstylist. It changed my life changed in the midst the storm. Pastor Denise, for all that you did and said, I'm eternally grateful.

Ms. Cookie, you and your "magic cap" made my confidence increase in one day. God gifted you with this ministry and your devotion to it speaks volumes. I saw many triumphs in your hair salon. You are a beacon of light to all who encounter you. Your hands are blessed and the love you display through them makes you a true legend.

My Sista, Sista, Lady Sherrell L. Hicks. As I write, the memories flood my mind. However, I go back to the initial phone call after the diagnosis. I can still hear that conversation now….that moment when you began to speak life over me, and told me that "we" were in this together. You took care of Christian immediately, held my hand while my hair was shaved off, and you made me *rest* when I did not want to take my superwoman cape off. Thank you for your commitment to our SISTERship and being consistent. My Cora!

My spiritual mother, Reverend Barbara J. McClain, you were there from day one. That was the day of the diagnosis and I had to speak at your conference that same day. You were patient and kind. You gave me the Word of the Lord that sustained me and helped me to understand my assignment in this *Life Interruption*. You helped me overcome the shock of the letters from *funeral homes* by reminding me of the promises of God. You were faithful to your role in my life and consistent in our relationship.

To my sisters, Denisa Burns and Jewell Gaskin you both cooked, ministered, made sure my holidays were good, looked after my son and husband, checked on our marriage, and made sure I finished strong. You were true spiritual sisters. I value you both.

To my three children; Mommy loves you unconditionally. Evan and Chloé Sophia, you are my two miracles after the storm. To my eldest son, Christian; you were there through this journey at age two. You kissed my bald head unexpectedly and that gesture was always on time. I'm sure you don't remember this, but know you were my little trooper and somehow, we had a flow. During that time, it seemed like you snuggled with me more, and you had patience for my weak and tired moments. I'm glad you came into my life and proud to be your mother.

To Chris, my husband; my love, no one has loved me like you did then and you do now. I don't know another man who could have walked this out with me. You love like you said you would in our marriage vows. You saw your superwoman wife become weak and tired, my highs and lows, the changes in my body and a bald head, but you chose to stay. You did not cheat on me, you did not find a mistress, you did not resort to anything that would damage us and our family. You were responsible, consistent, and I know for a fact you love you some *Carlette*, and I love me some *Chris.*

US

CONTENTS

ABOUT THIS BOOK

This book is broken into four sections. The first is the overview, the second section is our love story, the third section is our life interrupted, and finally the fourth section is restoration and a look at the actions we took until Carlette was pronounced cancer free. I believe the actions we took strengthened our marriage, brought us closer to God, and ultimately cured the cancer. If you are chosen for such a journey, it is our prayer that this book along with the steps we have taken will provide strength, inspiration and healing as you walk through the process.

PREFACE

Chris

I found the perfect wife. The icing on the cake was that we shared common Christian values. Although, it seemed as if I was going to have the perfect family, and near perfect life, it was interrupted when the "C" card was dealt to us.

Our family dynamic quickly took a turn, and although battling my own emotions, I had to adjust and step in to fulfill the duties that were typically handled by my wife. Although my battle was different from Carlette's, I still found myself vulnerable, broken, and desperately seeking answers.

I pray this book sheds light on the only ONE who is truly in control. Throughout our cancer journey, God gave me the peace to understand that He had it all under control. He is the one who gives sight to the blind, heals the sick, and causes day and night to come. God is in control and if we only could trust Him during times of uncertainty, our testimonies would be much greater. It was faith coupled with patience that caused us to overcome that cancerous time.

Finally, I am concerned for the men that do not have a voice. The men who are stuck behind the scenes while their wives, who, by no means am

I making light of their situation, are glamorized with such things as slippers, spa days, manicures, pedicures, speaking engagements, 5K walks and little pink ribbons. I know this may sound selfish, but it is my truth. I felt lost and confused.

Learning to lean on the shoulders of others often takes the greatest strength. For me, the struggle was real. There was not an outlet for me to get stuff off my chest to someone who could relate to what I was going through. On occasion, I'd have outburst, and my words were not always gentle nor kind. I had to check myself and realize that my actions stemmed from repressed emotions. Unable to truly articulate my feelings and not having a male support group for men whose wives had to undergo such an ugly battle was difficult. I now know that God pushes us into purpose, purges us, and develops our callings through fire. There are many things that are being birthed through this experience. One is the book you now hold in your hands.

I've learned that no one is exempt from life's difficulties, problems, or challenges. And needing the confidence, safety, and empowerment from men who understand one another is neither emasculating nor weakness. Recognizing that we are here to aid one another toward growth, healing, development, and Kingdom purpose is powerful. Pretending that we do not need others doesn't prove strength. In fact, true strength is found in the ability to lean upon others.

In this book, I open my heart, life, and most intimate moments, to reveal myself not as a hero, but a man fragmented by time and circumstance. And as a man who has learned surrender because of grace. As you thumb through the pages of this book, my portions will probably cause your emotions to vacillate between anger and sympathy. But whether you read from a heart to understand and learn or with a critical view, I must be veridical to my own experience.

It is imperative that you grasp how great God's love is for us, that even when life gets interrupted, He is God amid the intrusion.

My experience in walking through my wife's battle with cancer isn't isolated, but vastly unique. Each experience is different, therefore, I felt sharing our story and my part of the journey would be beneficial to the men who needed someone they could relate too. Transparently, I open my heart to share my fears, hope, courage, and strength.

During my research on couples enduring cancer, I discovered that some partners develop addictions and in some cases the strain of the illness causes marriage to end in divorce. I pray that this book will serve as a gateway toward emotional healing and maturity. I pray it deepens your faith in God and your marriage is strengthened all the more. Pay close attention to the action steps at the end of the book, they will serve as a great resource for you.

I stand in agreement with you this day that "…all things work together for good to them that love God, to them who are the called according to his purpose" (Romans 8:28 KJV).

The following Scriptures were anchors to my soul. Hold onto them and allow them to steady you during life's detours.

"Greater is he that is in you, than he that is in the world" (2 John 4:4 KJV).

"Knowing this, that the trying of your faith worketh patience. But let patience have her perfect work, that ye may be perfect and entire, wanting nothing" (James 1:3-4 KJV).

Carlette

Why did I write this book? The real question is why not? People need to hear another side of the cancer story. This is our story, my story — a story with a different outcome and some very unusual experiences. It is a testimony of what God can do through the power of prayer. I was challenged to look beyond the test and say yes to God's assignment. I would charge you to do the same. See the "Bigger Picture." God can use you to touch the lives of many. Chosen to be a living epistle may require a lot, but the reward on earth and in heaven is much greater.

"I remain confident of this: I will see the goodness of the LORD in the land of the living" (Psalm 27:13 NIV).

FOREWORD

Life happens to everyone. Events happen that we never planned or expected. We rarely get any warning or notice. No email, text message, letter, or phone call is received to prepare us for life's interruptions. Life just happens. Life happens to mature us, to develop our character, and to expose what is in us, the good and the bad. The comforting thing about life's interruptions is that even though they surprise us, they never surprise our Father. He is our Good Shepherd, and He always goes before His sheep. By the time we get there, He has already been there, and He has prepared the way for us.

If you allow them, life interruptions will teach you how to trust the Father, even when the way seems dark, hopeless, and uncertain. The Father knows the way that He takes us. We have a God, who can see clearly in the dark, during life's nights.

Life interruptions lead you on a journey. There are lessons to learn on the way and blessings to receive along the journey. There are many blessings along the way, they are not waiting on you at the end of the process. So, don't be so anxious to get to the end and miss all that God wanted to do in and through you throughout the journey. Some blessings are received while you are in the midst of the fire. Therefore, don't allow life's interruptions to overwhelm you, but trust the Father, and watch Him give you beauty for your ashes. He knows how to bring good out of the most horrific circumstances.

Thank you, Chris and Carlette for sharing your Life Interruptions with the world.

—Dr. Terence A. Merritt

Chapter 1

UNPROCESSED PAIN
CHRIS

"That's why you have cancer anyway!" I shouted, and like a slow-motion video, I walked back into the kitchen. Not realizing the full extent of my words, everything jumped back to reality. I felt like a bubble popped inside of me. Emotionally, my heart was crushed. The weight of the world seemed to be upon my shoulders as I burst into tears and ran into our bedroom. Still angry, I slammed the door. Soon after, the words that came out of my mouth began to haunt me. If there was ever a time a person put their foot in their mouth, it was that time for me, and I was afraid to face the backlash of my words. I stood motionless.

"The words of the reckless pierce like a sword, but the tongue of the wise brings healing"
(Proverbs 12:18 NIV).

I felt like "cancer" was robbing me of my place. I am the provider and the protector, and I found myself in a zone where I could not protect my wife, and I could not provide the remedy for what was wrong. I was broken. I quickly realized the pain that ill-spoken words can cause

1

and how easily they can flow out of the mouth during times of unsurmountable pressure.

How did this happen to her? to me? to us? I tried to transparently share my heart with others. I searched the internet for a support group for men and found none. I reached out to leadership who I thought would offer encouragement, a word from the Lord, or something. Up until this point, I'd been Carlette's superman. It felt like just yesterday we were walking down the aisle and beginning a beautiful journey together. We'd just experienced the birth of our first child and suddenly, things shifted. Our life was interrupted!

Unforeseen and unpredictable circumstances can throw us into a whirlwind. Without warning, I was left feeling empty and helpless. With screams that were inaudible to anyone's else's ears, I often drove alone in the car trying to deal with the pain. My heart is always to support my wife with every breath in me, and I just wanted…to…fix…it.

Going back to the beginning…

One night, I was playing around in bed with Carlette and I accidentally bumped against her left breast. She recoiled from the sharp pain. As she explored the area on her breast, she discovered a tiny lump. Carlette didn't think it was serious or anything to worry about, but for some reason, I was a bit more concerned and finally she agreed to at least get it checked out.

Five months later, we went to Gary, Indiana to visit friends. Among those we visited, was a good friend of Carlette's, Dr. Okechi Nwabara, who was a physician at

Methodist, South Lake Hospital in Merrillville. I casually brought up the pain in Carlette's breast. Dr. Nwabara asked her a few questions, and referred her to another doctor in Hammond, Indiana.

We called that office, set an appointment and went to visit the doctor. I can't remember his name, but I remember the office well. It was an older office building, very uninviting and cold. He told Carlette in a very uncompassionate tone, that she had stage two cancer. I really didn't know what that meant nor what the treatment entailed, but at that point, I wanted Carlette to get a second opinion. She agreed.

We went back to Indianapolis, and her OB doctor referred us to Dr. Timothy Goedde. I was at peace, though not fully aware of what was really going on or about to transpire. Lost in my own thoughts, I sat and pondered if there were any natural remedies that Carlette could use to heal herself.

After the results from the biopsy were in, we went for her follow-up appointment. He told us it wasn't stage two, but it was stage three cancer. I was shocked, confused, and anxious. One doctor said stage two, another said stage three, silently, I wondered what was going on? I jumped into rescue mode and instantly began researching the internet for natural care remedies. I couldn't bear the thought of her having her breast cut off and going through chemotherapy. I was sure she could live and be cured from cancer naturally. All kinds of thoughts ran through my mind, as I tried to figure out how she'd gotten cancer in the first place. Was it caused by our environment, food, or pollution? How did this happen? Was it hereditary? What were the steps toward recovery going to be? In the back of my mind, losing her seemed unthinkable. It was not something, I wanted to consider. Therefore, I chose healing and focused on helping her find natural remedies.

When the time came, I accompanied Carlette to see Dr. Goedde. His office was completely different than the first doctor we'd met. It was modern and inviting. The waiting room was friendly, with a warm ambience. Dr. Goedde was very thorough, and clearly explained to Carlette the steps he planned to take. First, he would do a biopsy, then, if it came back positive, he was going to recommend an oncologist. He was crystal clear, if it was malignant, the tumor had to shrink by chemotherapy. We accepted his advice and set another appointment.

When we met with Dr. Goedde again, it was after the biopsy came back malignant. He referred Carlette to an oncologist and told us we'd have to start radiation. Additionally, she'd have to undergo test to be sure that her heart was strong enough to cope with the chemo. He also set a consultation for us to meet with Dr. Bhatia. I thought he was a very funny guy. He was an Indian doctor, slender, 40's, vibrant and nice.

He explained the surgery procedures and told me that I'd have to take over all the household duties. Carlette and I both looked at one another and gave quirky little smiles. He wanted me to know in advance that Carlette would have mood swings, and hot flashes. He continued to explain things to us and then asked if we wanted to have more children? We both replied with an overwhelmingly, "Yes!" The doctor wasn't sure if he'd be able to save Carlette's ovaries, but he said that he would try.

At the time Carlette was five classes away from completing her master's in business administration. She was pleased to hear the doctor say that she did not have to stop attending her classes. The severity of the situation still had not hit me. In my mind she was okay. Somehow it was still a fog, or either I was deeply entrenched in denial. I've learned that denial is a process of grief. And maybe I was already grieving the thought of her losing her breast, not having any more children or worse. Nonetheless, I kept pondering the natural remedies that I read about.

Looking back, I guess I feel a bit dumb, because I did not grasp the gravity of it soon enough. As Carlette's husband, I guess a part of me, just wanted it to be done and over. I'd read somewhere that cancers were caused by pH balance being out of whack, so my thought was, "Okay, let's just get your levels back on track holistically, and we'll be good!"

After coming home one summer afternoon and pondering the thought of not having any more children, I felt a little scared. It was finally sinking in, and I knew I had to do something. Upon the recommendation of a holistic nutritionist, I purchased a set of pH balance sticks and some herbal tea that was supposed to help shrink cancerous tumors. Since cancer lives and grows in an acidic environment, I felt the important thing was for me was to test Carlette's pH level and have her begin a natural care routine.

As I walked into the house with my self-care remedies, I began to feel a bit more confident. I had my idea of us and our future swirling around in my head. Therefore, the need for me to help in any way that I could, placed a huge burden upon my heart. I put the store bag on the island in the kitchen and began to take items from the cabinets in preparation to make the tea. I took out a glass, spoon, and my wife's new Pampered Chef pitcher. I had to point out the kind of pitcher it was so that you would understand her aggravation even more. Those things aren't cheap!

I admit the tea looked and smelled horrible, but it was worth the chance. My goal was to create a non-acidic environment where the cancer would have to die. As I walked over to the couch where Carlette was seated, I positioned a test strip on her tongue. She was not reluctant at that point. I was very surprised at the result. It came back neutral. I wondered if this was a glimmer of hope for us, and my excitement grew. But as I gave her the cup of tea, she looked at me like I was crazy! It was a dark looking concoction and not very appealing to the eye. But I kept trying to get her to drink it. She refused the tea. We went back and forth for a while and I could tell we were both about to get very heated. We continued going back and forth. I was trying to help, and my convictions became even stronger that this was the cure that we needed. I was thinking...*If she'd only comply, we could get on with our lives.*

God's plans are often hidden in concealed places. And in this place, my eyes only saw one thing and that was her being free. Carlette remained stern. She stubbornly refused to drink the tea. We continued shouting and going back and forth and finally I caved. I gave up but not without uttering words that I didn't know could form on my lips. As I stormed out of the room, slamming the door, I shouted, "That's why you have cancer anyway!" Suddenly superman, was demolished by kryptonite. My hopes of fixing it came crashing down as I crumbled to the floor in a separate room.

After my tantrum, I was left out of the treatment decisions and although hurtful, I understood why. Right after the argument, I had ambivalent feelings. I didn't want her to have the mastectomy. I wanted to preserve her womanhood. I wanted what a man wants. (I know that seems shallow) But again, this is my truth. Men are very visual creatures. And maybe I was being selfish and didn't consider that she would be more affected

God's plans are often hidden in concealed places.

by this healing process than I would. Honestly, I was also very scared and worried too. I really didn't know what would happen throughout the entire process. The weight of fear, anger, hurt, and confusion, almost became unbearable, as the reality of cancer was finally settling in.

The Bible tells us to "Keep thy heart with all diligence; for out of it are the issues of life." I wish that I can tell you that I was a tower of strength and remained joyful throughout the entire process. I wish that I could say that I never worried or felt a tiny bit of trepidation. But that would not be the truth and it would not show my humanity. In the midst of displaying our greatest strength, we find that we are more fragile than we realize.

I do, however, wish that I would have fought my emotions and not let the situation get to me. I also found myself having difficulty at work. It was hard to concentrate, and I could tell that people really didn't know what to say to me about Carlette's situation. My pastor/boss seemed emotionless and carried on as if nothing in my life had changed. Carlette's name barely came up in our conversations and it bothered me because her health was always on my mind. He prayed with the team every morning before work but failed to mention her or "us" in the prayers. It was hard to believe because he was our pastor. My expectations could have been a little faulty, but it didn't set well with me. I understand that everything

> *In the midst of displaying our greatest strength, we find that we are more fragile than we realize.*

that happens in life is either God's perfect will or His permissive will, but it did not stop me nor my wife from needing encouragement, counsel, or prayers from our leaders. I can only recall the initial conversation when I first told him of Carlette's diagnosis that he was encouraging. I remember saying to him, "You never know what someone means to you, until something like this happens."

Every other time, he seemed to avoid the subject entirely. Dr. Sam was always kind to both Carlette and I, however, the depth of my feelings appeared to evade his consciousness. I felt that I knew his heart was concerned, but he didn't know how to express it. Nonetheless, it still left me with a bad feeling towards him.

After the argument with Carlette, I went along with her decision for surgery and chemo, but I felt left out in discussions of the surgery and reconstruction. I still wanted her to do homeopathic medicine. I was trying to do everything I could to help, but it became difficult when she no longer wanted my assistance. I knew that I deserved being shut out of everything after my actions towards her, however, shutting me out pushed me into a deeper shell of woundedness. Although I didn't feel emotionally involved in the process, I prayed and believed for Carlette to be completely healed. I can compare it to when my son Christian was born. I feared seeing all the blood and stuff, but I was excited about him being born.

I often took long drives and reflected on my marriage and my son. As tears flowed down my face, I decided to trust God even more. In addition, I am very thankful that we had health insurance. With the rising cost of healthcare, I felt blessed that much of the treatment was going to be covered by insurance. I thought about all the people without health insurance and my heart went out to them. As tears continued down my face, I bowed my head and whispered, "Thank you Lord."

Carlette

"And the LORD said unto Satan, Hast thou considered my servant Job, that there is none like him the earth, a perfect and upright man, one that feareth God and escheweth evil"
(Job 1:8 KJV).

I started working for our pastor who owned a dental office, as the assistant business manager. That title included being his personal assistant. I kept up with his calendar, scheduled and booked his meetings and his speaking engagements. I was also responsible for monitoring the sale of his books and mailing them out.

Wanting to fulfill my own personal dreams, I signed up for the MBA program at the University of Phoenix. The University of Phoenix professor asked us to write personal letters to ourselves as a way to stay focused and encouraged to achieve our goals. It was a "why am I doing it letter." I began my letter with, "Eighteen months from now, when I achieve my MBA, my life is going to change for the better for me, my husband and our son."

THE STEPS OF A RIGHTEOUS MAN ARE ORDERED BY THE LORD

In November of 2005, I went to a women's conference in Los Angeles, sponsored by a well-known Evangelist. It was the first night of the event and the minister of music told us to introduce ourselves to a person we didn't know and to share one thing that the Lord has done in our lives.

The lady sitting next to me seemed to be tired and I could tell the loud music was disturbing her a little. I also noticed that she was sitting while everyone else was enjoying the worship music. So, I took my seat and introduced myself. I told her to give her testimony first and afterward I would share.

I had no idea the information that she shared would be God speaking to me in preparation for the journey ahead. I'm amazed when I think back and remember this like it was yesterday.

She said, "I came for a word from the Lord all the way from New York. I just completed my last chemotherapy treatment for breast cancer. I am a Survivor!" After she spoke those words, I was so moved by her strength to make the long journey from the East Coast to the West Coast after completing chemotherapy, that tears filled my eyes. I hugged her gently and the testimony I was prepared to share escaped my mind. Instead, I told her that I would praise the Lord for the both of us. My praises to God were raised even higher.

In the months that followed, it seemed like I kept hearing sermons about the story of Job. I knew that I was about to face something but had no idea what it would be. Neither did I know that the strength of that woman's journey would soon be met by my own story of cancer survival.

Immediately after that four-day conference, I returned home and Chris and I were lying in bed, he was moving around and his hand brushed up against my left breast. I screamed from the pain, and immediately grabbed my breast. I began a self-examination. Feeling around the area, I felt a small pimple that I thought may have grown from an ingrown hair. Based on what I was taught concerning breast cancer, I expected the lump to be larger and not accompanied by pain. Therefore, I dismissed it, as nothing more than an ingrown hair.

Well about five months passed and the tiny pimple like lump was still there but the pain was gone. While visiting our relatives in Gary Indiana we made a quick stop to see my close friend/mentor Dr. Okechi Nwabara at the hospital where he worked. Can you imagine my surprise, while in a jovial conversation, Chris decided to tell Dr. Nwabara that I hadn't seen a doctor about the lump? Dr. Nwabara's countenance changed instantly and he quickly pulled out his script and wrote orders for a screening back in Indianapolis. He made me promise that I would move on it urgently. I promised, and within two days I decided to go to Planned Parenthood to get a quick exam because my regular doctor's schedule was full for the next several weeks.

The nurse that gave me the breast exam felt the lump immediately and was adamant that I go to my doctor as soon as possible. I called and told Dr. Nwabara and he stated for me to see his colleague who was a general surgeon and that he could see me within a week. Therefore, I made arrangements with my job to go back to Gary, Indiana to see the doctor. When I walked into his office, the atmosphere was cold. The walls and floors were all white, with no sign of life. The furniture was black and silver.

After the consultation with my husband and I, the doctor stated that he could remove the cancerous lump the same week. He also said it was necessary that I get an ultrasound and a biopsy. We agreed to the radiology and the biopsy but refused the surgery because we decided to get a second opinion.

After getting the ultrasound and biopsy, I walked out of the biopsy surgery with my left arm bandaged closed to my chest. My chest had ice packs taped down under my breast where the incisions were. I recall laying on that cold table for the biopsy, feeling like nothing more than a piece of meat. The support navigational nurse was not present at the time of the biopsy, which left me feeling a little uneasy. And even though they numbed the area, I could still feel the long needle. With each incision, warm tears flowed down the side of my cheek into my hair. When the nurse finally appeared, the procedure was over. I didn't acknowledge her but walked out hopeful, optimistic, and expected a clean bill of health. I was reciting Scriptures in my mind about healing being the children's bread and telling myself not to fear because God was with me.

To my surprise, my parents and oldest brother along with his wife were outside in the lobby waiting for me to come out.

The next day we went back to our home in Indianapolis; however, while I was at work the doctor called me and wanted me to come in his office to discuss the results of the ultrasound and biopsy. I notified him that we were two hours away and that we would have to discuss this over the phone. He was reluctant to do so, therefore, I knew the news was not good.

He, then, told me it was stage two left breast cancer. I was sitting at my desk on the phone when Chris walked into my office and saw the look on my face. I immediately told him and the color in his face seemed to fade. Chris left the office to tell our pastor, Dr. Sam. However, this was not just any day, this was also the day I was scheduled to be the speaker at a ministry conference. All kinds of thoughts flooded my mind. I started thinking of everything I had going on in my life, starting with the speaking engagement. I quickly called the ministry host of the news to tell her that I could not be the speaker for that evening.

However, about one hour before the engagement was to start, I went to the sanctuary of the church alone to pray. I turned on a song by Shekiniah Glory entitled "Yes." I cried and wept with my face to the ground before the Lord.

I had little words but many tears. I did not ask God why? I just cried out telling Him to help me. Before I got up, I told the Lord I will not accept this illness, but I will say yes to the assignment. The Bible story of Job came back to my remembrance. I then told the host of the event where I was scheduled to speak, that I would in fact continue forth as assigned. And she was glad because she did not have time to find a replacement.

We went to see Dr. Timothy Goedde for more test. He called me with the results, stating that the results came in and I was positive for breast cancer, and it was stage three not stage two. I didn't know the difference in the stages and had a lot of questions. I didn't want anything sugar-coated; I wanted the truth about what I was facing. Dr. Goedde told me to come into the office as soon as possible so that we could discuss my options.

He asked if I could come the next day and mentioned at my age 30, I shouldn't have to think about cancer. I arrived the next day with Chris for my appointment. It was the first week of April when I walked into his office. Pink was everywhere. I felt like I was coming into his life's work. First, he checked me out. He wanted to make sure I was strong enough to go through the process he outlined. As he examined me, it felt like a cold metal flame touching my soul. Doctor Goedde went into greater detail. He explained, ". . . This type of cancer is called Group 3, HER2 positive which includes tumors that are ER negative and PR negative, but HER2 positive. Your type of breast cancer, HER2 breast cancers, are likely to benefit from chemotherapy and treatment targeted to HER2."

Chris and I looked at one another. I wasn't really sure what all of it meant, but I knew I needed God's help and God's grace, because I intended on beating this.

He continued, "Now that we've completed the biopsy, and know what you have, this is the course I recommend." I listened intently, almost not believing this was happening. I felt like I had an invader inside of me. He continued, "The first phase of treatment will be chemo, I will see you every other week for about four weeks, and then, we will increase it to once a week, and follow up with radiation."

I asked him how long did he think the entire process would take? But he couldn't answer for sure, he just said that it would be probably be two years. This was all foreign to me, but I trusted that God had a plan for me, and that I would get rid of the invader in my body, because honestly, that's what it felt like.

Chapter 2

BEAUTIFUL BEGINNINGS

CHRIS

The hands of God masterfully weaves the tapestry of our destinies. I met Carlette through a co-worker, Wilette Blakely, who is also her cousin. One day while speaking to Wilette on the phone, she mentioned that her cousin was visiting and that I might be interested in her. She gave Carlette the phone as my heart began to beat faster and faster not knowing what to expect.

Trying to cover up my nervousness, I sounded very chipper and funny. As the conversation progressed, we agreed to meet on September 1, 2000 at Daren Blakley's house, who happened to be another one of her cousins. I knew then that she came from a large family and one that protected her at all cost.

I drove up to Daren's house, and he came out to size me up. He asked a few questions and then went to get Carlette. As she walked toward me, I could see that she was a beautiful young woman. It was as if she was walking in slow motion. Carlette was tall with long hair that hung below her shoulders. She was slender with an athletic build. She was wearing a black sleeveless dress and had the most beautiful smile I'd ever seen.

They say first impressions are lasting; and I was completely blown away! She was confident and very down to earth. I liked that she was also spiritual and valued her relationship with the Lord. During one of our conversations she told me that she was a church girl and a member of Revival Center Church of God in Christ. I know a lot of people say that they go to church, but the light of Christ was evident in her life. Before meeting Carlette, I spent a lot of time reflecting on the events of my life and I could clearly see the hand of God orchestrating my steps.

The evening of our first date was a typical 'Indiana' summer night. I was at church preparing my first sermon as a preaching minister. It took longer than I anticipated and was running behind for my first date with Carlette. I was rushing and didn't have time to properly get dressed for our first evening out. Since I was already late, I didn't want to go home first, therefore, I arrived in my very casual attire, and invited her to come back to my place with me so that I could get dressed for our date. She agreed. She was absolutely breathtaking, and I thought I'd lose my cool and confidence in front of her. I felt awkward and self-conscious. But her actions reassured me that everything was going to be okay.

I was silently praying, "God if this is the one for me, make her feel comfortable in my home." When we arrived, I escorted her in and noticed how comfortable she seemed. She even took the liberty to move my shoes and put them into the TV room.

I whispered, "Thank you God."

I was so excited to be with her. We decided to go to Lincoln Park, and on the way, I stopped by my parent's house to introduce Carlette to my family. Both, my mom and dad came to the door. My dad was all smiles as he told Carlette that she was pretty.

With a cute but polite response, Carlette said, "Well, thank you!"

The evening was going great and I could tell Carlette liked my parents. She conveyed in a later conversation that she enjoyed meeting them and admired how spunky and good-looking they were. My dad's sister lived across the street with her two sons, so I took her over to meet the rest of the family. I felt like I had known her forever even though we were on our first date. My aunt and my cousins were very impressed with Carlette. I went through a painful divorce and I could tell everyone was happy that I'd finally met someone who made me smile. They could see the sparkle in my eyes. I'm not sure how anyone else would have felt meeting the "whole" family on the first date, but Carlette was pleasant and seemed to fit right in.

After that, we headed toward Lincoln Park. I was still wondering if Carlette was the "one?" She was different. There was a synergy in our connection. Carlette was easy going, fun, and relatable. She made me feel very relaxed. I knew that I was safe with her. She was easy to talk to and I could openly share my heart. As the evening continued, eventually, the subject of my being late came up. She mentioned that it wasn't a good look for a "first date." I wasn't sure if I should tell her about the sermons but I decided to take my chances. I looked into her eyes and told her that I'd been working on my first two sermons and lost track of time. She smiled and asked to read them. I was elated by her request, but before I could hand them to her for review, she made a cute remark.

"You're forgiven for being late."

Carlette read the sermons and expressed her thoughts. She was encouraging and liked what God impressed upon my heart. Her approval reinforced my feelings about her. The evening flew by, and I knew she was like no woman I had ever met. We talked and laughed for hours. I felt like I was a new person and my personal dark ages had ended.

Where it all started...

I was raised in Gary, Indiana, and was blessed enough to be born into a loving, God-fearing middle-class family. I grew up during the years of the steel industry's decline. The city was named after lawyer, Elbert Henry Gary, who was the founding chairman of the United States Steel Corporation. Gary was steel, and so were its people.

The town's people held on as Gary experienced a drastic loss in population, which fell by fifty-five percent from its peak of 178,320 in 1960 to 80,294 in 2010.[1] At the time, it was considered the crime capital of the U.S., but my recollection is completely different.[2]

---

1 https://en.wikipedia.org/wiki/Gary,_Indiana *Bureau, US Census. "Population and Housing Unit Estimates Tables". The United States Census Bureau. Retrieved March 18, 2021.*

2https://en.wikipedia.org/wiki/Gary,_Indiana *Engel, Pamela (June 20, 2013). "Gary, Indiana Is Deteriorating So Much That It May Cut Off Services To Nearly Half Of Its Land." Business Insider. Retrieved April 6, 2014.*

To me, it was a city of proud, hardworking, kind, and hopeful people. I remember as a child looking at the horizon with the silhouette of the steel mills' long brick stacks billowing out white smoke, creating a haze in the distant sky. Occasionally, the earth rumbled from the banging coming from the mill. Everyone knew and respected my parents because my mother taught in the Gary public school system and was a part of a few social organizations including Delta Sigma Theta Sorority, Inc., and our family attended church on a regular basis. My father was known for his football skills at Roosevelt high school and his boxing abilities inside and outside of the ring. My older sister was proud of me, and always protected me. Her and I were always together.

The church I attended, St. Timothy's Community Church, was probably the most influential church in Gary. My great grandfather, Luther Moore, built and financed the first St. Timothy's Community Church, therefore, our roots at the church went deep. St. Timothy's was the pillar of the community and a staple in providing great job opportunities. Sunday morning worship was filled with the most influential people of Gary, Indiana.

We had a nice home. It was a good-size white brick ranch style home on a corner lot. From the sidewalk, a long white concrete walkway led to the front door with a large yard, which my dad always meticulously maintained. I had lots of room to play and grow. Everyone in the neighborhood greeted each other by name and wished for the best even in the worst of times. The streets of Gary also allowed me to have fond memories of my maternal grandmother's restaurant named Mae's Louisiana Kitchen. It was once located at 1814 Broadway in the heart of the city. Mae Bolton was known for her gumbo. One taste and you were hooked. People came for miles just to get a taste. Also, affectionately known as Mae's kitchen, it became a home away from home for many well renowned artist and activist. Some that I remember were; Nat King Cole, Dr. Martin Luther King Jr, boxer Joe Louis, actor William Marshall, and singer Ella Fitzgerald.

My paternal grandmother died of colon cancer in 1986. She was in the hospital and I went to visit her right before my freshman football game. I remember telling her that I was going to score a touchdown for her that same night.

Like all grandmothers, she was proud. That night, I forgot the quarter, as my dad was in the audience watching intently. Our opponent was in punt position. I rarely played special teams but that night I was in on the punt return squad. I was positioned on the outside of the line. They hiked the ball and one of my teammates blocked the punt. All I could see was a loose ball tumbling on the ground, and I had a clear view to run and pick it up to score a touchdown. After the touchdown, as I carried the ball off the field, all I could think about was my grandmother and what I had promised her.

As we celebrated the victory, my dad was grinning from ear to ear. Later that night when we arrived home, my mother told me that my grandmother passed away. I felt crushed inside. But I believe to this day that she waited until I scored to make her transition.

In 1996 my dad was diagnosed with prostate cancer. He had it removed at Mayo clinic in Wisconsin. Realizing how cancer affects people, I remember going down in the basement and praying for him every day. I strategically prayed, "God heal my father. Heal my parents, spiritually, mentally, and physically." Praying in this order was important to me. Spiritually was first, because I believe we must first have a relationship with God. Everyone must know that He is the One that will save us from sin and death.

I prayed secondly for mentally—mental strength and acuity—because our faculties must be in a good state. Our mental state is vital to every part of our being. Thirdly, my prayer was for healing of a physical nature. My maternal grandmother died from Alzheimers disease and I did not want my parents to go through that or any other illness. Their health and longevity of life for them were important to me. Therefore, I intentionally and strategically targeted my prayers.

During the year 2000, my father was diagnosed with breast cancer on his left side. This again was troubling for me because I did not want to see my father suffer, endure surgery or have health challenges. I believe that my consistent strategic praying was pivotal to their being alive and well enough to be here today enjoying their grandchildren. One of the Scriptures that I stood on was

Acts 10:31, "He told me, 'Cornelius, your prayer has been heard, and your gifts to the poor have been noticed by God!'" (NLT)

Carlette

It's very interesting, I had a dream about my future husband a year before I met Chris. In the dream, I was at a dinner with my parents and a man. I saw his face in the dream and realized that I knew him from college. The four of us were walking to our cars, and there was a puddle of water on the sidewalk in front of my parents. The gentleman took his jacket off and laid it across the puddle so that my mother would not get her feet wet. He helped my parents and I across the water and then, he said to them, "I am going to take care of your daughter."

As I stated before, in the dream it seemed as if I knew the young man from college. I also knew that he was a member of Kappa Alpha Psi Fraternity, a former football player, and a fair-skinned black man. I woke up the next morning happy and excited that God gave me a glimpse into my future mate and some of the qualities he'd possess. This dream gave me hope, especially since it seemed my past was full of losers.

A LITTLE ABOUT ME...

Up until the age of nine I was raised in Gary, Indiana. Then, we moved to a small town, Michigan City, Indiana, which is known as a tourist city. There were ice cream trucks in the summer evenings and children's lemonade stands. I played a lot of double-dutch and hopscotch. I was the middle child and only girl. My stepfather was a Pastor. We were a family filled with faith — Pentecostal Faith. God was never far from anything that I did.

My cousin, Wilette, worked with Chris, and set us up on a blind date. Wilette is the daughter of my mother's oldest brother, William. Being ten years older than me, she was like a second mother to me. She was also my friend, shoulder, and my rock. Wilette thought Chris and I would hit it off, and she was right! After talking on the phone, we agreed to meet at another one of my relative's homes.

It was about a thirty-minute drive to the house, and my cousin Daren was there. He was like another brother to me. I arrived early, and I wore a black sleeveless dress for the occasion. I was calm. I glanced at my watch and realized that Chris was late. About ten minutes later, Chris arrived. I liked him the moment I met him, and I could tell that he also liked me.

My cousin who is ex-military, checked him out completely. Chris didn't object to the line of questioning and that spoke a lot about his character. After the formal introductions, Chris asked me to accompany him to his house so that he could change clothes. Some people would have found this request to be strange, especially on a first date, but I was very comfortable with Chris. Besides that, my cousin knew where he worked, and everyone in my family gave him the thumbs up. I followed him back to his house, and he invited me in. He led me to the TV room and asked me to wait. I sat down and moved his shoes out of the way. I was really relaxed in his home.

Chris was very sweet. He was really trying hard. Still, I carefully observed his words and actions. After Chris changed clothes, he wanted me to meet his family. It was at that moment that I knew that he was serious about me. A short time later, we arrived at his parent's home. It was a very beautiful home. Being the gentleman that he is, Chris opened my car door, and we walked to the front entrance. His parents met us at the door.

Chris's parents were a good-looking couple, spunky and upper middle class. I could tell they liked me, and I liked them. I also noticed the kind, respectful, and loving way he interacted with his parents.

Next, he took me across the street to meet his cousins. I remember they offered us cold drinks and were very funny. We said our goodbyes and hopped back into the car. We discussed our date plans earlier, so I knew we were headed to Chicago. Chris suggested Lincoln park, and I agreed.

We had a wonderful time at the park. It was a perfect evening. The weather was comfortable, and I finally asked him why he was late, and he told me that he was at church and was working on his first two sermons as a preaching minister. I asked to read them, and he smiled. I read his work carefully and loved everything he'd written.

I could feel his vulnerability as I read. His words were from a man of deep faith who had been tested. Afterward,

I felt a strong spiritual, emotional, and physical connection to him.

He was in tune with his emotions and mine. I really didn't want the night to end. We talked for what seemed like an eternity. I told him about my past and he shared things about his past as well. The more I listened to him, I knew he was the man from my dream. I discovered he played football in high school and was a member of Kappa Alpha Psi. I felt like I'd found a long-lost friend, and like we had known each other forever. Not wanting the night to end, and in order to get extra time with him, I quickly told him that I wanted a polish sausage from Jim's Original off Roosevelt Road in Chicago. We drove there, and I only cost him $3! Now that was a cheap date. I had no idea that my life would never be the same after that night.

Chapter 3

ANSWERED PRAYERS, FAIRYTALES, AND DREAMS

CHRIS

I was always very attentive whenever Carlette and I spoke and spent time together. I took note of everything that was special to her. I wanted the evening of my proposal to be sentimental, heartwarming and a complete surprise. I involved those closest to her, including her boss. He was kind enough to arrange her schedule so that she'd be off that day. Although I swore everyone to secrecy, one person almost let the cat out of the bag. I'm glad the secret wasn't revealed. I also included the restaurant's waiters and staff so that the evening would flow perfectly.

I knew the restaurant on the 95th floor of the John Hancock building in Chicago held a deep meaning to her therefore, I chose it as the place that I'd propose to her. When I picked up Carlette, I couldn't take my eyes off her. She was stunning. Everything about her was an answer to my prayers. I was very nervous throughout dinner. I tried to play it cool, so as to not give any suspicion as to my impending proposal.

The restaurant had a spectacular view of Chicago and the lake shore. After ordering and finishing dinner, the waiter brought over the dessert plate. He opened the cover and the ring was underneath. I placed the ring on Carlette's finger and asked her to marry me. There was silence...

I didn't know what to do or what to think...I swear there was fifteen minutes of total silence between us. Fifteen minutes seemed like I'd stepped into the twilight zone. I was stunned...nervous...scared...and breathless. I wondered what she was thinking.

Finally, she looked over at me and said, "Yes." I was elated!

LET ME GO BACK, THE STORY BEHIND THE RING... .

On Wednesdays, we'd visit the church I attended for Bible study. I dropped her off and told her that I'd be back. I went to Kay's Jewelers in Merrillville and purchased the ring. I guess you could say I'm a bit old fashioned, because after purchasing the ring, I went to Carlette's parents to ask for her hand in marriage. Somewhat nervous, they asked me all types of questions, but later said yes. I wanted them to know that I was serious and showed them the ring to influence their decision. I did the same with her brothers.

I left Carlette waiting the entire time during the purchase of the ring and asking her parents for her hand in marriage. When I got back to the church, she was with our minister. I knew she would probably be upset but I didn't have a choice. And just as I thought, she began questioning me about being late? I really couldn't tell her the truth and ruin the surprise engagement. Without outright lying, I managed to convince her that I simply got tied up running errands.

After the engagement, we dated for six additional months and worked hard to get everything ready for our wedding. We also went through marriage counseling with two different ministers from different age groups. One was with Carlette's uncle. He is an older gentleman, who shared a lot of wisdom with us. The younger minister was my God brother. The counseling was serious, interesting, and insightful. We appreciated both perspectives and gained a lot from each of them.

Carlette's uncle was poised, serious, seasoned and sincere, also very straight forward, whereas, my God brother was energetic, playful, and hopeful. It was like getting meat, potatoes and dessert! That was the best way to describe our counseling session.

I was ready to get married when the big day came. I knew this was the person God ordained for me. We were married May 19, 2001. It was an exquisite day, seventy-five degrees, sunny with a beautiful blue sky. We had a large wedding. I think there were over two hundred in attendance. My cousins, Carlin Gray and Giovani Johnson showed up late to pick me up. Never- the -less, they got me to the church. I was so ready to say "I do," that I was dressed and eager to go when they arrived. All I could think about was how good God was and how much I truly loved my woman. I even got a little teary eyed as she walked down the one hundred-foot runner. Her makeup was flawless, and her wedding gown accentuated the curves on her body. With each step my heart skipped a beat. I couldn't believe that all my dreams were finally coming true.

Carlette

I was raised Pentecostal and Chris, non-denominational. We Pentecostals like to sing, and our services are vibrant and spirit-filled. I was grateful that Chris adjusted.

A month before the engagement, I was working at the Clinique counter, when a bouquet of red roses arrived. I opened the envelope, and the card read:

"Hello Carlette, these past few months have been amazing. I am grateful that you are in my life." The last sentence read, "Will you, ..." Signed, Chris.

I still didn't have a clue about what was coming up, because I thought it was too soon for him to pop the BIG question. I'll never forget what happened the day Chris purchased the engagement ring. We drove back from his sister's house in Wisconsin. Three hours was quite a lengthy trip. After arriving into Gary, he dropped me off at his church for Bible study and zoomed off. He didn't stay for Bible study and I thought that was very strange. A little perturbed I thought, *How dare you!?*

The minister there was very kind and kept reassuring me that Chris would be back soon. It seemed like hours passed while I waited. He was truly trying my patience. It wasn't until after the engagement, that I found out that he was out buying my engagement ring.

About a week before Chris proposed, a friend at work asked me if I had any good news? I didn't know what she was talking about. Later, I learned she almost blew the surprise.

Prior to the engagement, Chris was bugging me to take Sunday, December 3, 2000 off from work. I was on the schedule, but my boss suddenly decided to give me the day off. It seemed strange, but I quickly called Chris and let him know that my schedule changed, and we could go ahead and plan the date. Chris always made sure that our date nights were well thought out and special. It showed that he really listened to me and took note of everything that I liked. I should have known he was up to something when I was suddenly approved for the day off.

On December 3, 2000, Chris picked me up and took me to dinner at the John Hancock building, on the ninety-fifth floor. The restaurant held a deep significance to me. When my mother and father divorced, I hadn't spoken to my dad in years. When he did come back into my life, I was an adult. He took me to the same restaurant as a child, so it was very sentimental and special to me. It is one of my fondest and strongest memories of my dad, especially since his passing.

I guess you could say that I am sort of a daddy's girl. I cherished every moment I could get with him. I remember taking twenty-five cents of the dollar that my mom gave me to put into the Sunday collection plate to call my dad. I look back now, and realize, it was God's grace, because no matter where he was in the country, I seemed to be able to find him. I found him in Tacoma, Seattle, and Portland with a quarter, a payphone in the church's basement, and operator assistance. I asked his family and they would tell me where he was when they last heard from him.

The 3rd of December was also my father's birthday. Because Chris was so attentive, he knew all of this. He listened intently as I shared my heart and family history. It was heartwarming to know he included each detail in our engagement. Chris honoring my deceased father, further told me how incredible the man God blessed me with truly was.

When we arrived at the restaurant, with my eyes widening, I asked Chris if he was sure he wanted to spend the money to eat at such an expensive place? (Keep in mind, I didn't know the proposal was coming). Chris just smiled and escorted me in. I think we ate chicken with chili sauce for dinner. Both the food and the view were spectacular. The restaurant overlooked the Chicago skyline and it was decorated in a classy modern style. I vividly remember Chris wearing a black suit, white shirt, and a tie. After we finished dinner, the waiter came over and offered us dessert. I said no to the dessert tray. But moments later, he came back and asked again. Agitated I commented to Chris that if he came back again a third time, the dessert was going to be on the house!

After some small conversation, the waiter came back again with a dessert tray covered with a silver dome. I looked at Chris like I couldn't believe it! Chris knew that he was going to propose and was silently hoping I didn't blow it by going off on the waiter. With the finest from a polished food handler, the tray was in front of me on the table and he slowly removed the dome. Underneath were lilies surrounding a tiger lily, and on top of the tiger lily was an engagement ring. The tiger lily was the last flower I received from my father before he died.

The engagement ring was a one carat, marquise-cut diamond surrounded by diamond baguettes set in gold. I couldn't believe it. I didn't know how he knew, but it was exactly the ring I had dreamed of.

I never told Chris about the dream God gave me before I met him. I kept it in. I was still speechless as Chris began talking. He asked me to marry him and told me to think about my decision. He said there was no turning back, this would be forever.

He looked into my eyes and asked, "So, what's your answer, do you say yes?"

I was still shocked and overwhelmed as the words flowed from his mouth. I was speechless for about fifteen minutes. It was an incredible moment for me. I remember Chris, the waiters, and the restaurant guests staring at me.

After the engagement, the next six months flew by quickly. Either, I'd drive up to Gary from Michigan City or Chris would drive down to visit me. The synergy between us was perfect. We connected on all levels. My dream was true. It hit me a week before the wedding when I was sitting in church. I can remember exactly where I sat on the second row. His pastor Bishop Norman J. Hairston Jr. was the guest speaker at my parent's church, and they asked Chris to introduce the speaker for the evening.

Before Chris sat down from the introduction, he proclaimed his love for me in front of the entire church congregation and said this phrase while looking at my parents, "Don't worry I am going to take care of your daughter." In the dream he said those exact words to my parents. I was overwhelmed at the beauty of God to reveal to me in such detail His future plans for my life.

The day of the wedding I was up early. Wilette cooked breakfast for us and I didn't really want to eat. I remember her making me laugh by saying, "You don't want to pass out at the altar, and have everyone see your big ole feet poking out from under your big puffy white dress because you didn't eat any eggs!"

My Maid of Honor and I arrived at the church at ten o'clock. We were the only two there, even though the whole wedding party was supposed to be there at ten. The deacon was there and opened the doors to the church. I went to the bridal suite and watched the time. We had the rehearsal dinner on Thursday so that everyone would have an extra day to get things done.

The make-up artist arrived very late and sashayed in at 11:00 am. By that time, I'd applied my own make-up. I held my emotions together until my Godmother (my wedding coordinator) walked in and emphasized that things were supposed to start at ten o'clock, and asked where was the wedding party? That pushed me over the edge, I was so angry and upset that I burst into tears. My Godmother held my face, as I cried and said, "Don't do it." She cleared everyone out of the room, and said, "This is your day to be happy."

At that point, My Godmother, Rosalyn Wilson, asked everyone to leave the room which left only four people besides me, Claire, Wilette, my Godmother, and my maid of honor.

Claire fluffed out my dress, while the other three helped me get into my gown.

Chris and I were married on May 19, 2001, in East Chicago at the Faith Temple Church of God in Christ. By my Uncle, Pastor, and Chris' God-brother, Norman Hairston in our family's church.

Faith Temple Church of God in Christ is a historic building. With white brick exterior, wide steps that lead to a set of beautiful large wooden doors surrounded by nice landscape of flowers and trees. The interior of the church is even more beautiful. It had stained glass windows on both walls, light golden wooden arches which held up a white v-shaped ceiling, thirty or forty pews, with a center aisle. The walls were white colored and partially paneled. The white ceiling in between the wooden arches seemed to magnify its height. Colored light poured into the church from the stained colored panes.

Our guests and family members started to arrive. Chris's family sat on the left side; my family sat on the right. The church was packed, and the ceremony was scheduled to start at noon.

At twelve fifteen, I was still in the bridal suite preparing for my grand entrance. My wedding dress was a white ballerina dress, like the Vera Wang dress that I saw with a cathedral train. I wore my hair up.

I could hear the musical prelude coming from the church, which told me everyone was being seated. I was thinking about Chris, but I was still angry. Chris and his cousins arrived at the church late, and it was about twelve-thirty when I headed to the vestibule of the church to walk down the aisle. The music changed and in front of me, I could sense that the wedding attendants were in precession.

Our Kenneth Copeland Ceremony was so beautiful. The church was filled with both families and friends, and I could feel the Spirit of our Lord as soon as I entered. A joyous high energy filled the large room. My stepfather sang an original song as he led me down the aisle. There were tears flowing from the pews.

Chris' pastor was blessing, praying, and preaching it up! The organist even got into the spirit as shouts of hallelujah filled the crowd. My nephew, little Jay, was the ring bearer. He started falling asleep at the altar, because the praying went on for such a long time. My stepfather led me next to Chris and gave me away. Chris looked spectacular in his black tuxedo.

Then my uncle said the prayer:

"The marriage union is the closest relationship that can exist between two human beings. When a man and woman decide to join together in marriage, they should do so with full realization of their responsibilities."

We listened closely as he continued, *"Marriage is serious business. When two born-again believers know it is God's will for them to marry, they come together before God, a minister and witnesses to join their hearts and lives. They make a public profession of their mutual love and devotion, pronouncing vows and pledging their lives to each other."*

I took a deep breath…

He continued, *"As they pronounce the marriage vows in faith, the power of God goes into operation and a miracle takes place. They are united by God and become as one in His sight. Their union is threefold: They are joined together spiritually by God, legally by the contract they enter into and physically, when the marriage is consummated. A husband and wife are joined together as Jesus is joined to the Church. It is a miraculous union."*

I looked at my uncle as he presided over the wedding. I glanced over at Chris to catch his expression, and then looked out at the audience. I knew our Lord was joining Chris and I at that moment. I remember the moment so vividly, after the vows, pronunciation and our kiss, I stood in awe as I looked at our guests. We both beamed with joy. We prepared to take our photos and head to the reception.

The reception was a typical Pentecostal reception. It was held at St. Timothy's. One hundred and sixty guests came. Baked chicken smothered in sauce was the main course with rice and green beans served on bone china.

Our wedding cake was a five-tier white cake with lemon butter creme icing. It was delicious. A photographer from the corner snapped pictures. Randall Blakely was our D.J. and Chris's six fraternity brothers sang the Kappa sweetheart song. I remember Fred had a great voice. All the wives came up and welcomed me into the family.

The reception tables were covered with our plum and silver wedding colors and highlighted with Calla lilies. I chose Calla lilies because the Calla lily is associated with holiness, faith, and purity. Additionally, as the Calla Lily flowers blossom in spring, they have become symbols of birth and Christianity.

After the reception, we stayed the night at home. The following day, we visited Chris' parents and left for our honeymoon in Las Vegas!

Chapter 4

FOLLOWING THE VOICE OF GOD

CHRIS

We honeymooned in Las Vegas for two weeks. We walked up and down the Strip, ate exotic foods, stayed at the Bally's, and took in a lot of shows. It was a joyous rest from the pressure, tension, and excitement of the wedding and all of the planning.

I knew Carlette really loved me when she was ready to come to my defense. As we were walking into one of the casinos, I accidentally bumped into a lady as she was walking out. The lady looked back at me as if she was going to do something. Carlette turned around and looked at the lady as if to say, "Don't try nothing with my man, cause I'll cut ya!" I smiled inside and giggled to myself. I looked at her and held my head a little higher. When we returned from our trip, we jumped right back into the normal routine of going to work and settling in as a married couple.

A year later in September 2002, we moved to Indianapolis. Prior, to moving, we met a minister through an old friend of Carlette's. She invited us to a church there in Indianapolis. After visiting the service, we both felt that God was leading us to connect with the ministry.

The connection was also felt by the leaders of the church. They asked us to pray with them. It was the most amazing prayer, and it catapulted our relationship with the Lord. We couldn't shake the church from our minds, hearts, and spirits. I really felt I was led to help the ministry. I asked God, if we are supposed to move?

I also asked Him to give us a sign. Later that day, I decided to put out a fleece like Gideon, and if I heard the word Indianapolis that same day, then it would serve as the sign that I needed to move forward. I went to work and the first customer that came in mentioned the word "Indianapolis" in his first sentence. I felt that was the answer to my prayer and a sign. After speaking with Carlette, we made plans to move and dedicate ourselves to broadening the message and ministry of that little inner-city church.

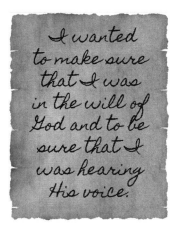

The move to Indianapolis was the first time that I can say God began revealing things to me in a prophetic way. Just Like Gideon, I wanted to make sure that I was in the will of God and to be sure that I was hearing His voice. In the biblical narrative of Gideon, we find Gideon seeking guidance from God. Read Judges 6:36-40:

"So Gideon said to God, 'If You will save Israel by my hand as You have said — look, I shall put a fleece of

wool on the threshing floor; if there is dew on the fleece only, and it is dry on all the ground, then I shall know that You will save Israel by my hand, as You have said.' And it was so. When he rose early the next morning and squeezed the fleece together, he wrung the dew out of the fleece, a bowlful of water. Then Gideon said to God, 'Do not be angry with me, but let me speak just once more: Let me test, I pray, just once more with the fleece; let it now be dry only on the fleece, but on all the ground let there be dew.' And God did so that night. It was dry on the fleece only, but there was dew on all the ground."

After being sure that we'd heard from God, we connected with the pastor of the church. He also was a dentist and also owned the oldest black gospel record label in the city. I felt led to join and assist him in ministry.

In 2002, on August 23, which happened to also be Carlette's birthday, a company that she applied to in Indianapolis called and offered her a job. It further solidified the fact that we were following God. As a bonus, it was a great birthday gift!

Carlette started her new job in September and we went down to look at homes. We viewed several homes and finally fell in love with a townhouse that overlooked a pond. It had two bedrooms upstairs and the kitchen, living room, and dining areas were on the first floor. It was light and airy with a nice ambience. And even though it was near a busy street, the road it was on was quiet and residential. We filled out the application, and after getting turned down, the rental company changed their mind, and the townhouse was ours. To me, it was another sign. So, we packed and said our goodbyes to our families and friends. We headed to Indianapolis.

We started attending Dr. Sam's Church, every Sunday, which was located on the East Side of Indianapolis at Thirty-fourth Street and Scoffield, and I became the Administrator of his dental business around the corner.

I started putting in long hours, working and helping with the ministry. The church was in a high crime and drug area. At the time, it had the highest rate of HIV in the nation. Being in the inner city afforded us the opportunity to evangelize and do a lot of outreach. The church centered around meeting the needs of the community. We served and ministered to alcoholics, drug addicts, homeless people and families suffering from abuse, poverty, and neglect.

Serving in outreach pushed me out of my comfort zone and gave me a deeper understanding of living by faith. Dr. Sam had strong faith in our Lord, and a very distinctive look, almost regal. He was a man with a very thin frame, nearly bald, and had a reflective personality. He was calm in persona and demeanor, very conservative, humble and stood about five foot seven in height. He lived in a gated community, but his home was modestly decorated. He had a deep sincerity for the Gospel.

The church itself was in a nursing home that also had a halfway house inside of it. For five years it served as our place of worship and employment. I grew a lot under his tutelage. And learned a lot about faith, hope, and compassion.

Over time, I could feel my experiences being transcended into wisdom through faith. I was grateful to be there, and very grateful to have a spouse who trusted me as I in turn trusted God.

Our relationship and our marriage deepened and strengthened. It was a great time for us. We were immersed in our faith, one another, the ministry, and our work.

With all major tests of your faith comes opposition. People said that we should not move to Indianapolis. Others even questioned if I truly heard the voice of the Lord? I didn't back down but stood firm in my decision. I knew what God was leading me to do. And as a result of our obedience, God was opening the right doors.

THE BIRTH OF OUR SON

The next big event in our relationship was the birth of our first child. I took Carlette to Community North Hospital. And after a long time in labor, the doctor told us that Carlette would need to have a C-section because Christian's heart rate was dropping. At the time, I think

With all major tests of your faith comes opposition.

there were five people in the room, Carlette, her mom, the doctor, a nurse, and me. I am not good with needles. I was so nervous that when the doctor informed me that I would have to change into surgery scrubs to go into the room with my wife, I immediately dropped my trousers. Sadly, it was in front of my mother-in-law.

The anesthesiologist asked me to hold Carlette still while he gave her the epidural, or she could become paralyzed. After seeing the blood and the needle, the room started to spin. In the nick of time, Carlette's mother came to my rescue before I passed out! Once the medicine set in, it was a waiting game. But as time passed, Christian's heart rate continued to drop. The doctors and staff rushed to get Carlette into the operating room. Finally, at 5:27 am, Christian was born. March 3, 2004 is a day, I'll always cherish. I remember seeing Christian's face for the first time. He weighed seven pounds, fourteen ounces and was twenty-one inches long. He was a healthy, happy, and if I must say, handsome boy. Carlette stayed in the hospital for five days. Her parents came to visit, and my parents came up that first weekend.

Life took on new meaning for us with a son. The next year went by rather quickly as we settled into a routine as new parents. Life was blissful!

Chapter 5

CALLED, CHOSEN, AND CONSIDERED

CARLETTE

After being a new mom for two years, I was diagnosed with cancer. The doctor informed us that the first phase of treatment would be chemo, then he would need to see me every other week for the first month. After that, they would increase the chemo to once a week and finally follow up with radiation. I wanted to know what the entire process would entail and what it's length would be? But unfortunately, the doctor couldn't give me a precise time frame. He said we would have to wait it out.

When the word got out that I was diagnosed with breast cancer, I was approached by two different individuals who both told me that I'd been afflicted with cancer because I had unforgiveness in my heart. It was hurtful to hear such statements, but in all humility, I asked God to search my heart. As if a person under extreme trial doesn't question his or herself enough, we are sometimes bombarded by people who lack true discernment with idiotic questions and statements. I was also asked what did I do to deserve this? In error, they really believed that I was being punished by God.

I'm convinced in our day and time that people really do not know how to discern an attack from the enemy, God's permissive will or discipline by God. These two individuals would not let up. They drilled me with question after question. Although one of them was worse than the other, both left me feeling completely drained.

I recall one instance where we were at church, and I was up testifying of God's greatness and how He brought me through. They stood beside me and whispered in my ears. In front of the church! They questioned me like crazy. I felt trapped and they made me think back, soul search, and almost convinced me that I was being punished. I felt smothered by them. They wouldn't let up or relent until I gave them a name or a situation. They kept pressuring me to tap into my childhood and really think back. I don't know where they got their theology or this tactic, but not everyone has the same situation. I finally caved and threw out a name so that they would leave me alone.

It's insanity, but that seemed to satisfy them. I guess they thought they'd done their job, by getting to the "root" of the cancer. I pray that deliverance ministers would truly seek the Lord in trying to help offer aid to others. I am aware that unforgiveness and bitterness can open doorways to the demonic as the Bible tells us in Matthew 18:34, but there were no lingering issues in my life nor unforgiveness towards anyone. I felt very defeated after leaving that church service. The best way to describe it was that my spirit was extremely grieved. I was unsettled and really disturbed by their actions. I felt unjustly condemned. During the moment that I needed them the most, they offered judgment and not comfort. I know that people mean well when they are trying to help but do not always have the wisest words nor actions. It is best to seek the Lord in prayer before immediately condemning individuals. Although I prayed hard afterward, I did not totally release it to the Lord because I was still feeling condemned and slightly irritated. I was downcast, until the Lord spoke very clearly to me and asked, "What did I tell you?" and He repeated Himself, "Have you considered my servant Job?" He stated, " I did not tell you that you had unforgiveness in your heart. Go back and read Job." I was relieved and followed His instructions.

I stood firm on the word of God. I then had to pray and forgive the two individuals. Once I did that, I regained my composure and posture. In ignorance, people can say some dumb and insensitive stuff, and although hurt by their actions, I knew I must forgive them and move on. I also knew malice was not their intent. They were simply doing as they had been erroneously taught. I had 'bigger fish to fry', as the saying goes. I was on a mission because I told God yes to the assignment, but not the diagnosis. So, those two folks were par for the course. I had to keep praying on my weekly prayer mandate and keep the story of Job in front of me, especially Job chapter 2.

ANGELS ON EARTH

The first night of chemotherapy, Chris had to be out of town for his job. I knew that if it wasn't for work, he'd be by my side. Therefore, I reassured him that I'd be fine, and he should go without harboring any ill feelings. Chris didn't want to leave me by myself and arranged for one of our church members to stay with me until he returned. Let's just call her Mrs. Barbara. Mrs. Barbara is a praying woman and I trusted that she'd have me covered in prayer. She was kind and very attentive. I was very grateful to have her stay with me during my first chemotherapy treatment. She saw first-hand the raw moment where hope and fear were vying for my attention.

I asked her to take me to get a wig just in case my hair started to fall out. I'd rather have been proactive instead of reactive. She knew I should probably rest and not be out shopping for wigs, and truthfully, I felt as though my body was walking down a flight of stairs. That is the best way I can describe it. I was ready to lie down and obey the command of the chemotherapy drugs. Chemo has many different side effects. For me, it was extreme nausea. It was worse than the most awful pregnancy nausea, and extreme fatigue. Indescribable fatigue. And earlier in the day with my pre-meds the nurse warned me of side effects of steroids, such as cravings. Well instead of sleeping in my bed that night, I chose to sleep on one couch and Ms. Barbara chose the other. At three a.m., I felt a gnawing in my stomach, and I knew exactly what was happening, but I thought I could just ignore it and go back to sleep. Well I fought for one hour and at 4 a.m., I screamed out, "I can't take it anymore, I'm hungry!"

Ms. Barbara literally jumped up from the couch out of her sleep to see what was going on. I kept repeating that

I was hungry and couldn't fight it anymore. She grabbed fruit and juice and the lion within was tamed. Now, just imagine my being alone in the house having this intense episode. I am sure that I would have called Chris and started screaming for food. Knowing Chris, he would have tried to get something delivered as soon as possible if not cancel his trip altogether!

Later that morning, we laughed as we recounted the hunger aspect of the medication side-effects. "A closed mouth never gets fed."

When the news went out that I was diagnosed with breast cancer and was undergoing full chemotherapy treatment, I began receiving numerous phone calls and well wishes. I was very comfortable with sharing about the cancer, but only for the purpose of prayer and speaking in confidence that the Lord had my life in His hands. I believed and stood firmly on the Scriptures. I held on to the Scripture at Psalm 118:17 which says, "I shall live and not die, to declare the works of the Lord." And John 11:4 which says, "This sickness is not unto death, but for the glory of God, that the Son of God might be glorified thereby."

Many churches prayed and sent love; however, one church in particular, did something that I will never forget. Pastor Harry Beard of the City of Refuge COGIC of Kokomo, Indiana called for a prayer and shut-in meeting at the church for an entire weekend. The entire congregation stayed at church all day and night to pray for my complete healing — in the 21st Century! I couldn't believe it.

Then, his wife, Lady Etiwanda Beard, sent fresh fruit and other delicacies that made me feel special. She made sure my cousin Sandra Bush, who was a pastor's wife as well, brought the treats on one of her many trips to Indianapolis. She also had her daughter call to check on me periodically, especially since she was a physician. Lady Beard was even planning on sending people from Kokomo to sit with me during my weekly chemotherapy treatments. What a Blessing! That was a true act of kindness and love. I appreciated their unselfishness to leave the comfort of their homes and beds to petition the Lord on my behalf.

It took no time for the chemo to have effects on my body. Namely, my hair. After the very first treatment in May 2006, my hair started falling out in clumps. I prepared myself by purchasing a wig after my first treatment. But nothing could have truly prepared me to see my hair fall out in massive amounts. To say that I was distraught is putting it lightly. The Bible says that a woman's hair is her glory, and I felt my glory fading away. I was facing a new reality. But I thought just maybe the hair salon would have an answer. I went with the hopes that they could do something to save my hair. My friend, Sherrell Hicks, was with me. I sat down in the chair, and as my hairdresser started to brush my hair, the middle started to fall out. She said she was going to shave it all off. I remember her crying as she slowly shaved the hair from my head. Sherrell took pictures so that I could remember that moment.

Chris

I was with Carlette and Sherrell (who met us) at the salon. But decided to leave them there and drive around the area while I waited on Carlette's call to tell me that she was ready. I was driving, when suddenly, my cell phone rang well before I anticipated and without giving to much detail, Carlette beckoned me to come back quickly. Anxiously, I headed back. When I walked in, I saw her hair missing in spots and I realized the chemo was starting to take effect on her body. I didn't want to lose it in front of her, so I held back my emotions and with a huge lump in my throat, I went to the car to grab my camera for Sherrell. Carlette and I both wanted to document the entire cancer process, therefore, we had Sherrell take photos for us.

It was difficult watching my wife endure such a painful process. It is very onerous to watch someone you love suffering. Cancer became even more real to me as I saw the effects that chemo was having on her body. I wanted to break but couldn't. I really needed the shoulder of someone who understood my pain. While I appreciated the ears of my close friends, I really needed so much more. It was a trying time and I leaned into God and my faith to strengthen me.

Carlette

It was a Friday when I purchased my first wig. That following Sunday, I went to Rock Community church at its new location. The pastor, his wife, and some other members were also there. No one besides my husband knew that my hair fell out and I was bald. I felt very strange and the wig felt like a huge hat! I kept thinking that my husband and son had more hair than I did.

Before I go any further, I want to tell you a little bit about my best friend. I met Lady Sherrell Hicks through my husband, who met her at the dental office. During one of their conversations, she shared that she had a church childcare facility called Open Door Church Child Care. Chris encouraged me to go view her daycare for the purpose of enrolling our son Christian a few months after he was born. I was on my way to a corporate luncheon but decided to stop by the daycare. I was told that I could drop by anytime for a tour, therefore, I made an unexpected visit to the daycare. Lady Hicks personally gave me the grand tour, and a packet that contained all the facilities information and her business card. After being extremely pleased, I was preparing to leave. When I got behind the wheel of my car, God began speaking to me regarding my connection to Lady Hicks.

After the luncheon, I called her and asked if I could come back to see her, and she obliged. When I returned to the office, one of the teachers excitedly thought that I was coming to enroll my son. I grinned to myself, because at that point I hadn't made up mind about the enrollment. I was just coming to share what I heard the Lord say. As I walked into her office and began to share what was on my heart, tears began to flow from her eyes. We both knew that it was God because the words resonated in her spirit as well. I had so much more to share, but the last statement that came out of my mouth was, "And I am going to help you."

The statement came out so fast, I was afraid that might have misunderstood God. I put my hand over my mouth in awe. Little did I know three to four weeks later, I would leave my job in corporate America and trade in my business suits to assist her in Child Care, wearing khaki skirts. I did the marketing, strategic planning and quality assurance for her company.

Our friendship grew and we were no longer formal, but on a first name basis. When I received the news from Planned Parenthood that they felt a lump, Sherrell was the first person that I called. She insisted that I get care immediately! Sherrell also began to speak the word of the Lord and pray. She vowed she would be there for me because she had also walked through cancer treatments with her husband a few years before my diagnosis.

When chemotherapy treatment began, she gave us free childcare for Christian, and kept him longer on the days I had a session. She was also kind enough to drive Christian home after going the extra mile to feed him dinner and put him in his pajamas. She was another one who made sure I had plenty of fruit, juices, and water.

I wanted our lives to be as normal as possible and would often push myself to do the same things that I did before chemo. One day, I was trying to be wonder woman after a chemo treatment and attempted to leave town for a ministry engagement. My husband was unsuccessful in trying to convince me to stay home and rest, so he enlisted the aid of Sherrell. He told her that I was being hard-headed and as I was dropping Christian off at her childcare facility, she came out of the building and literally pulled me from the car. She insisted that I rest. She told Chris to leave me there with her and said stated that she would take care of me. After leading me to her husband's office, and allowing me to rest on his leather sofa, she prepared lunch and checked on me throughout the day. My body really did need the rest. It was the best seven-hour nap I ever had!

It wasn't a coincidence that it was her that I attended that women's prayer conference in Los Angeles with a few months before the diagnosis came. And It's so funny that many have said that I favor her more than her biological sisters. We hear it all the time, people naturally assume that we are sisters. She remained by my side throughout the entire process and to this day we are still best friends.

HAIR CHRONICLES

Pastor Denise Carpenter heard about my survival of cancer and out of compassion she reached out to check on me. Her connection was truly God sent. She was affiliated with cancer survivors and knew how hard it could be on the body and self-esteem. During our many conversations,

I conveyed my dissatisfaction with the wig I purchased from the store. She referred a lady by the name of "Ms. Cookie" who made custom wigs that looked natural and set up an evaluation for us to meet.

Pastor Denise Carpenter accompanied me to my private consultation with Ms. Cookie. While I was waiting, my anticipation grew as I carefully observed the other women who came out looking fabulous after their hair appointments. Ms. Cookie's salon was in the basement of her home. The sign outside read, "Ms. Cookie's Cut and Curl." It was older brick home off of 38th street, a bungalow style two-story house. Ms. Cookie was patient and kind. When it was my turn, she told me to remove my wig. Tears began to flow down my face as I removed the wig. She reached out to comfort me and told me that this was her ministry. She was gifted and compassionate. She also told me that she felt all women should look and feel beautiful. I felt her heart and passion to encourage and empower women who'd been through cancer.

Ms. Cookie's business was known for, "The Magic Cap Wigs." Her technique isn't uncommon, however, her attention to detail and desire to see women evolve after cancer makes her process one of a kind. She customized my wig to fit my head. And after creating a hairline, she used bonding glue and a stocking cap, and the wig was made right on my head. She gave me highlights and styled it well. When I looked at the finished product, I could hardly believe my eyes! I felt very pretty and like a woman again. The style was so me, sassy and jazzy! Having my hair/wig styled by Ms. Cookie gave me hope. I felt like a million bucks! It is important for women to feel attractive; it boosts of our confidence and I truly believe it aids in the healing process. It also gives us the power that illness and chemo can strip away.

The gratitude I felt toward Ms. Cookie and Pastor Carpenter was hard to put into words. I was overwhelmed with gratefulness. So much more than a wig came out of that hair appointment. I felt more empowered than ever to beat cancer!

Chris

My wife's strength amazes me. She tackled cancer with grace and grit. Hair or no hair, she was and will always be beautiful to me. Despite the huge weight she carried, she'd still find joy in my comedic jokes. I'd compare my bald head to hers and she'd laugh uncontrollably.

I was glad that Pastor Denise Carpenter introduced Carlette to Ms. Cookie. Once Ms. Cookie designed a custom wig for her, I could see her spark coming back. Without the bulky wig she had at first, I could tell that she was less self-conscious and more confident. She was also more comfortable sporting a shorter hairstyle with a sassiness that matched her personality. We were grateful for Ms. Cookie.

Chapter 6

BROKEN AND BLESSED

CARLETTE

After the first session of chemo, I determined to move forward with my life. I went to church every Wednesday to pray for one hour between one and two p.m. I felt strongly that the Lord wanted me to go into prayer. However, I wasn't led to pray about my own situation, instead, I was led to pray for others. That time of prayer proved to be healing for me as well. In fact, I know that it helped me to heal even faster.

There were people who worked with me to stay accountable—The pastor, his wife and another sister in the Lord. I had a lot of responsibilities in the church and was committed to service. I oversaw facilitating Sunday school. I was a member of the praise team, leadership team, and was also on the Board of Elders.

The times for prayer were chosen specifically by God. I knew it was Him, because I wouldn't have given up my TV show otherwise. But it was such a strong unction in my spirit that I knew I had to be obedient! See previously, I was a faithful watcher of 'Matlock' and it aired between one and two o'clock in the afternoons, but I gave it up.

It may not sound like a big deal, but anyone who knew me and how much I loved that show, knew it was a huge sacrifice for me.

Obediently, I went to church the same time every day to pray. God will place us on assignment and we never know how our obedience will impact another person's life. I listened as God spoke to me and prayed for everyone that He laid upon my heart.

Additionally, prayer requests came in from people in the church and community. I'd pray over bills, photos, and all other concerns as the Holy Spirit led. I'll never forget one particular day, I walked into a store and a woman that I'd never met recognized me as the woman who was praying over her son.

Previously, she'd sent in a photo of him and stated that he was in prison. It was a heart-warming moment. I'd never expected to meet her, and it was truly an honor. She embraced me and fell into my arms in tears. She was grateful for the prayers and said that she'd seen a change in his attitude and faith. We praised God together.

People started coming at the same time to praise the Lord with me. God's spirit was moving heavily during that time, people were giving their lives to Christ and being baptized. I did this for the entire year of my chemo treatments. We'd worship, pray, and allow God to perform miracles. The power of God flowed through me and echoed throughout the church. Several people gave their testimonies and we all knew that it was a God ordained season.

Two Scriptures the Lord kept before me were, Job 42:10 and Isaiah 43:2. Job 42:10 says, "Job said, 'And the LORD turned the captivity of Job, when he prayed for his friends: also the LORD gave Job twice as much as he had before.'"

And Isaiah 43:2 says, "When thou passest through the waters, I will be with thee; and through the rivers, they shall not overflow thee: when thou walkest through the fire, thou shalt not be burned; neither shall the flame kindle upon thee."

I Knew God was With me!

As I stated, I wanted Chris and Christian to retain a level of normalcy. I'd push myself to continue moving forward. I love our date nights and wanted to us continue dating and courting as before. I typically had chemo on Fridays, so the morning before having my treatment, I told Chris that I wanted to go to dinner and see a movie. After dinner, I guess he could see that I was really exhausted, and he insisted I go home and go to bed. Normally, I'd persist, but he was adamant. I'm glad because I really needed to rest.

Brokenness

Before Chemotherapy, patients are given pre-meds to help combat nausea and vomiting. There was a series of four pills to be administered to me. The first two treatments were also the hardest treatments on my body. The premedication was given to me free the first two times, although money wasn't an issue. When it was time for the third round of medication, there was a co-pay of $75. I cannot recall why, but for some reason I did not have the $75. I remember leaving the pharmacy and I completely broke down. I guess it was a moment where everything that I'd been holding back, finally reached the surface.

There were no generic medications to substitute for a lower price at the time; it was brand name only. I hit a wall and the whole time of being strong came crashing down on me. I broke completely. I sobbed horribly! That moment was a great release for me. I needed to cry, I needed to scream, and I needed the release. I could clearly see how depression can find its way into people's lives during illness. I didn't battle depression, all Glory to God, but I understood how easily that door could be opened.

There are blessings in brokenness. It wasn't my strength but God's strength that kept me. And in one moment, needing that one pill and not having the money for it, triggered every human emotion possible. I'd reached a breaking point. But my brokenness was not beyond repair. God already knew that moment would come for me. And He in His infinite wisdom already declared that blessed are the poor in spirit [broken].

When we humbly admit our need, God's grace overshadows us. And because we do not have a High priest who cannot sympathize with us in our hour weakness, we can endure the trials that come to test us. Jesus knew the joy that awaited Him; therefore, He endured the cross. He willingly laid down his life. No man took it from Him. (John 10:18). All God ask is that we are willing to allow Him to break everything in us that is unlike Him, so that new life can begin. Only through brokenness, can God's abundant life be released through us to flow to others. He had a greater plan.

When we humbly admit our need, God's grace overshadows us.

When it came time for the fourth and last pre-medication, I opted out. I wasn't about to pay the $75 again, plus I already knew what to expect. That third time—the time that I hit a wall—fortified me, therefore, I prepared myself and prayed through the full side effects of the chemo without any additional medication.

The first four chemo treatments were horrible. They were very brutal and hard on my body. Once the treatments were over, there was no cancer found in my body. I shouted praises to God! I was relieved and thought it was done and over. But my journey was only beginning. The doctor said that I still had to go through the prevention phase so that cancer would not return. I didn't expect that. I was prescribed a softer drug to test to see if I could use it for the second phase. Tears filled my eyes. I was angry; no not angry, I was furious! The doctor noticed my demeanor. I was hurt, sad, and without me saying a word, he hurried and introduced me to a colleague. After he left, I cried as I spoke to the nurse. I was able to convey the things that I could not accurately articulate to him. Maybe because she was a woman, I felt more comfortable and felt as though she could sympathize with me. She encouraged me and told me that I was a fighter.

She said, "You are going to make it through. You won't be as tired, and you are going get your spunk back."

I was mentally exhausted. And I was ready for my hair to grow back as well. I cried in her arms. I was tired. I was even tired of the bald head. I felt that I looked like a man. I wanted to shout to the doctor, "I'm bald man! Come on!" It wasn't that he'd given me false hope when he told me the cancer was gone. I just took it to mean that it was over. But it was far from over.

ENDURANCE

During the second phase I wasn't sick. And I did not have to do the pre-medication. The third phase after surgery was preventative again. I had to do chemo for a gene mutation and hormone. The total process took about 15 months and was originally said to take two years. Glory to God He shortened the duration by nine months according to their speculations.

The day of the mastectomy was November 14, 2006. I was getting ready for surgery and the phone rang. It was our pastor who was also our employer. He asked to speak to Chris, but before I handed Chris the phone, I asked if he was calling to pray with me/us before surgery? He quickly stated that he was praying for me in his private time, and although it was not the purpose of his call, he would go ahead and pray. I handed the phone to Chris and listened to him ask my husband when was he coming into work to do the payroll? I'm sure as you are reading this, your reaction is the same as mine, upon hearing such a uncompassionate and selfish request. My mouth dropped! I was in shock, but I had to catch myself. It is times like these that your heart is truly tested.

I changed my attitude and focused on what lay ahead. I reassured my husband that I'd be fine, and when they took me back to surgery, he could go ahead and complete his job duties and come back to the hospital before surgery was over. I noticed Chris' countenance. I couldn't imagine the weight that was on his shoulders already at the thought of my mastectomy (the removal of my left breast), but to have received that phone call regarding work in the middle of what we were facing was outrageous. Chris appeared more subdued after that phone call, so I prayed for him to be calm and have peace during the process.

I put on a full face of make-up because I wanted those people to see that I was alive and well and not just another body to be cut on. I was taken to my pre-op room and I sat in the room alone. As I waited, I turned on my worship music and sang along to the song, *You Are Alpha and Omega.*

I was in worship mode and at peace with my eyes closed, and suddenly, I could feel people surrounding me. I opened my eyes and it was Chris, my parents, and a minister friend of ours. This young minister had zeal for the Lord and was unashamed.

He asked questions about how I was feeling, but it seemed as though I wasn't emotional enough for him. So, he asked if he could pray and I agreed. They all grabbed hands around me. The minister began to pray, and his zeal was coming through. He prayed very long and loud, and it seemed as though he would not give up until he saw tears, or he provoked an emotional response from me. I could just sense that is what he wanted. In disbelief, I was laughing on the inside and I mustered up a tear for him so that the prayer could be over, and it was over just like that.

The surgeon came in and gave us some last-minute information and encouragement, and I was taken into surgery. In the operating room Michael Jackson was playing and I giggled. The nurse wanted to know if the music bothered me, but I enthusiastically stated that it seemed like there was life in the room! It was an incredible feeling. We all laughed and gave one another high-fives.

Hours later, as I was in recovery, I opened my eyes to see my guest and worship just filled my soul. I began singing about how worthy the Lord is. Before long, I drifted back to sleep. I'd awaken off and on and try to speak to everyone.

My mother told me about the many visitors from pastors and their wives. They came from all over the city. She said it amazed her because she knows how busy pastors are. The fact that they took out the time to come just touched our hearts. They all wanted to see me open my eyes! Less than twenty-four hours after the surgery, I was about to walk out of the hospital, but the nurse insisted that I be wheeled out to the car due to hospital policy.

My sister-friend, Sherrell Hicks, drove me home since my husband was at the house getting things prepared for my arrival. I was greeted with fresh flowers and his warm embrace.

Sherrell has always remained a true jewel. She took Christian to daycare and brought him home. That kept the flow of his daily schedule.

In the beginning, when I was diagnosed with breast cancer, I was five classes away from the completion of my MBA. I told the oncologist Dr. Bhatia that I was not going to quit my studies because of the cancer diagnosis. I was determined that it would have to fit into my schedule, and he agreed that I shouldn't have to stop doing the things that I would normally do, but I needed to take breaks as needed. I vowed to myself that I would avoid telling my professors about it until I had received my final grade for each class. When class was over, they all asked the same question. "Why didn't you tell me?" My response remained the same.

"I did not want any special treatment and I wanted to earn my "A" like everyone else."

My final class was the culmination of my capstone project. I had to submit it exactly four weeks after the mastectomy surgery. I paced myself each day to work on it a little at a time, especially since I could only type with one hand. My left hand and arm were still bandaged and propped a certain way to avoid any injury to the surgical site. It was December 15, 2006 right before midnight that I turned my project in.

A few days later, I received my final grade of an "A" and feedback from my professor. He asked what were my plans since obtaining the MBA? I finally told him about the health issues and the surgery, but not before I gave him a huge heartfelt thank you! I explained how I persisted, and even typed with one hand to complete the assignment.

He wrote the following words to me, *"Congratulations! You were weighed. You were measured, and you were not found wanting!"* He stated that he would have gladly given me an extension, if I would have told him about the cancer and the mastectomy. But as I said before, I wanted to earn my "A" without any special treatment. I typed back, *"She Came. She Saw. She Conquered."* And I thought that was the end of our conversation, but his rebuttal was everything to me. He wrote, *"And She did Not Want for Anything and She Recovered All!"*

Post Operation

I never liked medicine, especially after finding out the toxins they release in the body. Therefore, I refused any heavy pain medicine and if the pain became to intolerable, I took regular Tylenol. One of the challenges of recovery was learning to balance my body weight. I had one breast and that caused the imbalance. I was previously very heavy chested or well-endowed and typically bought my bras from high-end department stores. As a double (H), It was difficult for them to size me with a prosthetic. But I finally got one with inserts. And one of my favorite things to wear was a tank top that had pockets to securely and secretly fit the draining bulbs inside. I'd wear it underneath my regular clothes.

Physical Therapy

The room for physical therapy was very serene. I enjoyed going, it was calming although sometimes the stretching would be painful. Once I felt the intended pop, I knew the therapy was giving me more flexibility. I couldn't move my arm above my head because of the removal of lymph nodes, so that was the goal in order to prepare me for radiation. My mom stayed with us for about a month to help us, and people brought us cooked food. We were very blessed. I was out of commission. I was supposed to be on rest for six weeks. By the fifth week I had cabin fever and went to church with my arm taped up and wore a shawl to cover my arm.

I made myself look in the mirror and face the reality of not having my breast. I wanted to face the actuality of it. And it was a true battlefield of the mind. I had to talk myself through the changes in my body. Insecurity, fear, and lack of confidence can take a toll on the mind, body, and spirit. The enemy was right there to compound the feelings by trying to make sure that my womanhood was challenged. I fought back fervently! I'd put on earrings, lipstick, perfume, and whatever made me feel sexy and like a woman. For a little extra motivation, I'd sing, *I Feel like a Woman* by Shania Twain and Whitney Houston's version of *I'm Every Woman* also helped.

Reconstruction

I waited a long time for reconstruction. Although the wait was draining, I discovered it was in God's perfect timing. Right after we moved to Georgia, I had Evan who is my first miracle baby since having breast cancer. The doctors advised me to wait two years before having other children, then he switched it to 5 years. It was exactly five years after my last chemo treatment that I got pregnant with Evan. Because of the cancer and the waiting period, I had to be careful and to avoid pregnancy, I had an IUD inserted. Once it was removed, I got pregnant in three days! It was a true miracle.

My doctor asked if I wanted more babies and the answer was no! We really thought that we were done. After seven years they weren't sure how my skin would snap back after having reconstruction surgery. But I was still willing to try. God is so Awesome. Our move to Georgia proved to be a true blessing. I was introduced to the co-creator of the TRAM procedure. The doctors and I agreed not to go as large in the reconstruction as I was naturally and previously. I really enjoyed the smaller size breast. I can't say the same for my husband though. He is a breast man, and before the cancer, I had more than enough as a size HH.

For me, it was true freedom from years of backpain and shoulder bruises. Chris didn't understand that it was more than physical appearance or a sexual fantasy. I'd battled for my life, and I was ready to be comfortable. Because of his insensitive comments, I didn't want him to go to the consultation with me. I'd had enough of him, and I couldn't take any more comments. I felt that he was being very selfish, and I was really upset with him. The doctors told me it was my decision and my choice if I didn't want him to come in the back as we discussed the procedure for the reconstruction. I told him no, and kept it moving.

During Tram they do a tummy tuck to take some of the belly fat to reconstruct the breast. It was the best procedure.

Chapter 7

LIFE INTERRUPTED (A NEW NORMAL)

CHRIS

As much as I wanted to shield Carlette from this painful experience, I had to move out of God's way and allow Him to weave the tapestry of our destinies. He was writing the story and I had to trust that He had our best interest at heart.

Grief has many layers—it is not tied to losing someone in death. We can literally grieve any kind of loss. Cancer took away some of the things that I loved. One was my wife's breasts. The other was time, plans, and life as we knew it. I'm a breast man, and it may seem selfish because my wife is the one who underwent the surgery and the chemo. She had to deal with hair loss and the loss of her breast, the physical and emotional exhaustion, along with the other symptoms of the treatments. As a man I cannot tell you exactly how she felt about her womanhood, but Carlette is a real trooper. Even if she was down, she would do her utmost not to reveal it or to even allow it to linger. After a day or two, she'd rise and be as spunky and sassy as ever. Seeing her strength encouraged me, but it also revealed my weaknesses. My weaknesses caused me to feel less like her hero and more like just a regular Joe. Of course, she never saw me as that; it was how I allowed the devil to make me lower my own self-worth.

When I saw other women with large breasts, I wondered *why Carlette?* I had no thoughts of being unfaithful to my wife. My vows were not because of marriage, they were because the love I have for her surpasses anything I've ever felt in my entire life. God has blessed me with everything and more than I'd asked for in a mate—I was overwhelmed at God's faithfulness to me. And as I mentioned in the beginning of the book, even her body was something that I loved. Her curvaceous figure, radiant beauty, kindness, compassion, humor and relationship with the Lord was the total package. I truly prayed that the enemy wouldn't toy with my mind nor my emotions to cause me to see other women as more attractive because of "breast."   I know the lure and trap of lust and seduction and fought to keep those things out of my mind and heart. I know this is difficult to hear, but I want to be completely open and transparent so that the men who read this, can draw from my experiences and know that they are not alone.

I want men to know that God can keep them faithful to their spouses even in trying times. The Bible tells us that, "Charm is deceitful, and beauty is passing, but a woman who fears the LORD, she shall be praised" (Proverbs 31:30). Faithfulness is more than not having a physical affair, as Jesus also warned us, "adultery can be in the heart." As Christians, we know that we are supposed to deny ourselves for Christ, but faced with conflict and challenges in our marriages, we forget that we "men" are supposed to deny ourselves for our wives. Carlette has always been my rock and now she needed me to be hers.

I was battling my own emotions, thoughts, and needs, amid grieving our former life. And although God's plans are great towards us, the painful process can seem anything but great. When our eyes are clouded by circumstance it is hard see God's hand masterfully weaving a beautiful portrait of purpose.

I wanted to say and do all the right things. I wanted Carlette to know that I was still attracted to her and once she was able, she and I continued our intimate relationship. I was nervous about the way she would perceive my response to her physical changes from the cancer treatments and surgery. I wanted her to know that my love would never change, and I didn't want conveying that to seem superficial. It was so much to consider that it weighed heavily upon me. By the way, never make jokes or harmful comments regarding your wife's body, especially during an illness.

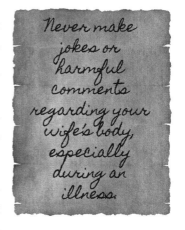

Never make jokes or harmful comments regarding your wife's body, especially during an illness.

I also felt a little envy toward other couples who were not going through such a strenuous process. It seemed as if our lives were on hold while everyone else's was moving forward. I wanted someone I could share my thoughts with. And I searched desperately for a support group for men whose wives had cancer and found none. Everything that I considered the "norm" was highly impacted by this cancer. Even at work it seemed as if people tip toed around the conversation of it, and no one knew the depth of my pain.

I was able to confide in my friend Reggie Lillie and he gave the best advice he could based upon his experience. But as a married man, I was torn between not wanting to disappoint my wife and not wanting to disappoint God. I wanted to authentically express my feelings without being judged and condemned. I was unprepared but also determined to learn as we went along. This wasn't just Carlette's battle, it was mine. We are a team. She was called, chosen, and considered, and so was I.

Chosen to walk alongside her on this journey, I knew that we'd have to depend upon God like never before. When Carlette lost her hair, I'd make jokes to keep her laughing and kiss her head. After she healed, I'd lay my head in the empty spot were her breast used to be and listen to her heartbeat. We still had fun and enjoyed one another's company.

When Carlette returned to our home after having the mastectomy, the marriage vows became very real. During this process, we also purchased and moved into our new home—a two story, five-bedroom, three bathrooms house on a cul-de-sac. We painted the downstairs in sage green and hot cocoa, and the upstairs in antique apricot. We were blessed to find the perfect home. Our new place was very bright and cheerful. We moved October 16, 2006, exactly one month away from Carlette having surgery and our son was two years old. I didn't know if I had unrealistic expectations or no expectations at all. After the surgery, I remember taking Carlette upstairs and placing her in the bed. She was bandaged from the surgery with both arms bound against her body. She had two drainage tubes with bulbs coming from underneath the bandages.

Every day I had to change the two drainage bulbs filled with fluid and blood. It was very tough to see my wife go through such agony and pain. I am not one for the sight of blood. Remember, I nearly passed out during the birth of our son but mustered up the courage to help my wife transition back into normalcy and heal properly. I put my best face forward, despite feeling helpless most of the time.

Besides working full-time, I also took over the domestic duties of the family, which involved cleaning the house, doing the laundry, fixing dinner, and getting Christian ready for school. This made me realize how important Carlette is to my life. I wondered how she managed to do all these chores, take care of our baby, maintain a job, get an MBA, and a continue in a full-time ministry?

I have always appreciated Carlette, but I gained a new and greater level of appreciation for her. I was very busy with work, and having a spouse with cancer, who was so young, was difficult for me. I couldn't quite grasp it. Carlette was healthy, confident, and strong. She barely took any medications because of the harmful toxins they leave in the body and took care good care of herself.

Contrary to "religious" thinking, I continued to grapple with *why?* Her facing cancer took the breath out of me. I mentioned in the beginning of the book that I wanted to take control of the situation and fix it. I thought by researching cancer and finding a solution to counteract the cancer, everything would be fine. Unfortunately, my quick-fix ideas proved to be useless. We had a process and God had already designed the road we would travel.

I tried to establish a routine, which was especially important for our son, Christian, and actually for all of us. Carlette dying from cancer was a fleeting thought. I knew God wouldn't take her from us, but there were periods where I wondered why Carlette? And why us?

Those thoughts assailed my mind more than I'd care to admit. I was also concerned about our sexual intimacy, future children, and the uncertainty of cancer's return. I realize the answer is not always in why? But rather why not? And more often than not, we are told never to question God.

Scripture is replete with biblical narratives of those whose questions rang aloud. Questions are not an indication of a lack of faith, they are more an indication of extreme pain and God is near to those crushed in spirit and brokenhearted.

Please consider the following three Psalms of King David and the words of the prophet Habakkuk, just two biblical characters who desperately sought the Lord for answers:

"How long must I struggle with anguish in my soul, with sorrow in my heart every day? How long will my enemy have the upper hand? Consider and answer me, O LORD my God; Enlighten my eyes, or I will sleep the sleep of death" (Psalms 13:2-3).

"I will say to God, my rock, "Why have You forgotten me? Why must I walk in sorrow because of the enemy's oppression?" (Psalms 42:9).

"How long, O LORD, must I call for help but You do not hear, or cry out to You, "Violence!" but You do not save?" (Habakkuk 1:2).

Their heartfelt cries to God show us that God understands human frailty. We all have questions from time to time, and I realize that the answers to those question still may not suffice nor take away the pain. There is also a chance that we may not get the answers that we desire. Even with that, we must not become embittered toward God. Knowing all of that, still didn't keep me from racking my brain concerning her diagnosis. I wondered if we'd made the right decision moving to Indianapolis? I wondered about our eating habits? If it were something environmental? If there were any areas where we were not obedient to the Lord? I've discovered that questions are normal, and they are okay.

It was aggravating that I could not find any resources for the spouses of cancer victims. I'd hoped that some resources or a support group could help answer some questions like, "What are some different ways I can help my wife?" and "How do I reference this disease?"

I felt guilty, because I wasn't sure what I should say or do. Carlette refused to say that she had cancer. She would only say she was "diagnosed with cancer." I struggled with always choosing the right words when explaining our situation, or even in simple conversation with Carlette.

I didn't know if I should ask how she was feeling or just say, it is so good to have you home. These may seem small, but it is really a huge deal. The wrong words can ignite emotions and allow the enemy to come in. I would have appreciated more resources to help me approach Carlette's cancer.

Also, someone told me that I should never ask how she is doing? But not asking seemed a bit uncaring. I was told to simply say it is good to see you and I love you. It all left me torn between not saying enough and saying too much.

I did know one thing, and that was, that I needed to trust the Lord. I also knew He never gives us more that we can handle. I just wished as a family, He didn't think that we could handle so much.

The time flew by, and Carlette continued staying positive and trusting our Lord. Her positive attitude and resolute faith helped me with my faith and attitude. Our marriage was growing stronger. Supporting, catering to, and nurturing my wife was second nature to me.

We are called to love our wives as Christ loves the church. Jesus gave Himself for the church, so loving Carlette and giving myself to her in every area is not only a duty, it's an honor.

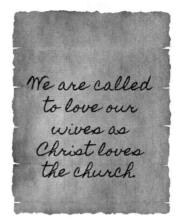

I decided to trust God daily. I needed to process things and take it step by step. If negative thoughts popped into my head, I determined not to give in to them. I had to understand that the actions were ours, but the results were up to God. When I got scared, I learned to give my fears over immediately the Lord. In doing research for writing this book, I discovered that men may feel more distress over the cancer of their wives than the wives themselves.

I tried to keep our family life as consistent as possible for all of us. I went to work, did the chores, took care of Carlette and Christian to the best of my ability. It was mentally and physically exhausting. That is another reason to surround yourself with people of faith. Those who agree with you in prayer, and not those who make you feel as if you aren't praying the right words or praying enough.

Our marriage and faith continued growing. In some ways, the greatest spiritual growth happens when we need God the most. I look back now and really think God carried us through that tumultuous storm. God gave me the idea for this book and to put together different resources, forums, and support groups. Not being able to find any support groups for men, I decided after Carlette's cancer was gone, I was going to do something to help other people in my situation.

I knew going into this we had a strong faith and a strong marriage. We also had the financial resources and good health insurance, to make sure that Carlette received the best care. At work most days, I found it difficult to concentrate. I would have preferred being home with her as she recovered, but we needed the money and the health insurance. I was grateful to have her friend Sherrell's continued love and support and that of many others.

I prayed nonstop! I also thought about the people who may have to face the same situation, without strong faith, solid marriages, or adequate health insurance. What do they do? Where do they turn? That is another reason for this book and our willingness to share transparently. We know that we were blessed continuously throughout this process. As God blessed us, please be assured, His loving arms will hold you through it all as well.

Conclusion

CARLETTE

It was the end of July 2007 when I went for my eighth week check-up. It consisted of checking my heart's ejection fraction to see if the chemotherapy had affected it. The results came in a few days later. I was already scheduled for another chemo session, therefore, when that Friday came, I didn't think twice about not having it done. I went in and Dr. Bhatia, the chemotherapy oncologist stated that my cardiac ejection fracture was low and that we had to give my heart a break for three weeks. He mentioned that we would re-test the heart ejection fraction at a later date.

Well, I returned after three weeks and was tested again. I went in to see Dr. Bhatia for the results. The wait at the Cancer center was longer than usual. Although the nurse came in to explain that they were unusually busy and it shouldn't be much longer, the wait continued. I finally told them to just call me and checked myself out.

While on the way home, I was listening to the gospel song *I've got a Testimony* and I sang along. I was no longer thinking about the test results, instead my focus was on the upcoming ministry trip, when I received a phone call from Dr. Bhatia.

He apologized for the wait but wished that I did not discharge myself. However, the test results came back concerning my heart. He stated that instead of the percentage increasing which would mean that it was getting better, it actually decreased in the ejection fraction. Which was not good. I thought we would have to wait another three weeks. However, he then said my body and my heart had enough. He said that I was done.

He ended the conversation by saying, "You are healed!" He actually said, "You are healed!" He didn't say remission, he said, "Healed."

At hearing those words, my mouth dropped, but I had to keep it together because I was in the middle lane of the highway. I was stunned it seemed unreal. And to make it even better, it was my birthday weekend! I called my husband and told him, and he rejoiced with me.

 That following Sunday we went to my parent's church and later in the service they wanted me to share some words. I gave my testimony that the process was over! My parents and the congregation went up in worship. But by Monday morning fear approached me just like it did in the beginning. I was wondering, *Where do I go from here?*

The chemo and doctor's visits had been my life for the past 15 months. The cancer was gone, and I'd completed my treatments. Fear began speaking loudly about cancer returning. But I was reminded of the Scripture that was given to me in prayer from Denisa, *"The Lord will fight for me and protect me and never leave my side" (Isaiah 43:2).*

Forged ahead in faith, my purpose came into full view. I became a nurse and as a cancer survivor, I began speaking at breast cancer functions, social events, women's groups and churches.

My story was featured in the newsletter for the Community Health Network of Central and was distributed to over 100,000 physicians and members of the network. I was also the recipient of the Sharon L. Bassett Foundation award-an award given to breast cancer survivors. I received gift cards, money, a monogrammed blanket, and a big beautiful gift basket. I was nominated by my navigational nurse Claudia Davis for obtaining my Master of Business Administration degree while in breast cancer treatment.

Chris and I began speaking at marriage retreats on the topic: *In Sickness and In Health.* I joined the American Cancer Society - African American group of BC survivors. With all of that, one of the most important assignments, was meeting one on one with breast cancer patients in current treatment.

Being able to encourage and pray for them made it all worth-while. I also had another miracle baby-Princess Chloe in March of 2017.

Chris

> "Trust in the Lord with all thine heart; and lean not
> unto thine own understanding. In all thy ways
> acknowledge him, and he shall direct thy paths"
> **—(Proverbs 3:5-6)**

I am reminded of this Scripture constantly. It serves as great empowerment as we face various trials. Looking back, Carlette's road to recovery seems like a brief moment in time. "For momentary, light affliction is producing for us an eternal weight of glory far beyond all comparison, while we look not at the things which are seen, but at the things which are not seen; for the things which are seen are temporal, but the things which are not seen are eternal" (2 Corinthians 4:17-18).

But when you are in trial, "light and momentary" can seem very far off. Carlette's battle not only made her strong and sharpened her ability to hear from the Lord, it made my trust and faith much stronger. Trust is one of those big-ticket items that I needed in order to make it through. I shared time and time again, how hurtful it was not to have anyone that I could call on who knew exactly what I was going through. I really believe a support system would have helped to reinforce my strength and faith. And while I know there was no support group for me, God almost, always uses the pain in our lives to birth through us what is needed in the earth. There was an assignment in this for both of us, only it took me a while to see the design of God at work.

There are some husbands who are unaffected by the physical changes that happen to their spouses during cancer and other illnesses. Unfortunately, I did not have a blueprint nor advance warning. I am mature and faithful enough to stand by my wedding vows, but that did not mean that I didn't need assistance in shifting my mind.

Although I leaned on the shoulders of my two buddies, I found a part of me was still empty emotionally. I needed to be around men who understood the full magnitude of what I was dealing with. I needed to understand if my emotions were fleshly or if something sinister and deeply spiritual was attempting to attack me in some un-regenerated areas? This was deeper than not having an ear or shoulder to lean on. I needed godly wisdom, counsel, and discernment.

As time passed, the purpose for our pain became clear. It was predetermined that I was chosen to stand beside my wife during this storm. The Bible tells us, "But without faith it is impossible to please Him: for he that cometh to God must believe that He is, and that He is a rewarder of them that diligently seek Him" (Hebrews 11:6).

Carlette often mentions this was a test that the Lord gave to her; however, because it affected me on a different but still painful level, I know both she and I were chosen for this. We have a testimony together, but also separately, God was increasing our faith, anointings, and ministries.

In fact, when I look back over my life, I can see how God orchestrated each step to increase my faith. From our first date-marriage-moving to Indianapolis, Indiana-the birth of our first child-the cancer diagnosis-losing both jobs at nearly the same time-relocating to Atlanta, Georgia then to Los Angeles, California. All of which have been defining moments in my life, that took as Dr. Bill Winston so eloquently states, "The God kind of Faith."

I've had my times of disappointments, disbeliefs, frustrations, fears, doubts, and anxiety, but it was faith in God that changed my unbelief to belief. The fact that my lovely wife, Carlette Nicole Edwards, is still a living soul, completely healed, and miraculously gave birth to not only one child, but two after having cancer is a true miracle and testament of faith.

"Now faith is the assurance (title deed, confirmation) of things hoped for (divinely guaranteed), and the evidence of things not seen [the conviction of their reality—faith comprehends as fact what cannot be experienced by the physical senses]. For by this [kind of] faith the men of old gained [divine] approval" (Hebrews 1:11-12).

The kind of faith mentioned in Hebrews 1:11, also says by this faith the men of old subdued kingdoms. It is this kind of faith that causes us to fully surrender to God knowing that He is in control. This kind of faith lets us know that whatever we lose, God has something greater in store and wherever He leads, He will guide us and provide for us there. If it had not been for the decision to give my life over to God, confessing Jesus as my Lord and Savior in 1999, my life would be a complete disaster. Faith in Jesus Christ has kept me. Romans 8:28 tells us, "And we know that all things work together for good to them that love God, to them who are the called according to his purpose." As I look back to the beginning of my story, I always reflect on the pattern of prayer God set when I asked God to heal my parents. The order was very specific and strategic. I mentioned this pattern in the beginning of the book-spiritually, mentally, and physically. I would like to offer you the same pattern of prayer to help you get through any challenge you may be facing.

The first order in the pattern is spiritual healing. It is the most vital part as all others will follow. When we are healed spiritually, our minds are renewed, and our souls can receive the wholeness that will change the trajectory of our lives. In spiritual healing we also gain a deeper connection to God, and can gain a clear understanding of who He is and all He desires to do.

He tells us, "If ye abide in me, and my words abide in you, ye shall ask what ye will, and it shall be done unto you" (John 15:7 KJV). The helplessness I felt while walking Carlette through the cancer journey was met by the power of God. I learned that He steps in when all human efforts are exhausted. I realized that my job was to take all the actions I could to help and encourage Carlette to stay positive and know the actions were ours, but the results belonged to our Lord.

I pray for the knowledge of God's will for me each day. And secondly, I asked God how I could best serve Him and my family? If I ran into a snag, I would write a list of ten solutions to the problem and try to implement them.

Sometimes we must take practical steps in addition to applying the spiritual guidance that is needed. At times the answer I needed was within the ten steps. At other times, I'd find that my human efforts were to no avail. Even in my weakness, God proved His strength was made perfect.

Wanting the cancer to disappear, would have removed what God wanted to do through us. It isn't that God purposely gave Carlette cancer to teach us lessons. We know that sickness entered the world through sin. God hates sickness as much as we do. He sent His only Son Jesus Christ to save and deliver us. However, God doesn't waste anything. He allows these circumstances to show His grace and teach us patience, love, faith, and to rely on His power.

Because of these test and trials we've grown closer to God and stronger as a family. Throughout this journey, I've learned there are no coincidences in life. Each person that crosses our paths are meant to be a part of our great destiny. Allow God to lead you and know He will make all things work together for your good. Everyone has a story that is unique to the path that God has ordained for their lives. When we allow it, our stories bring Him Glory.

ELEVEN ACTIONS TO RECOVERY

Looking back, I realize I was developing a faith walk with our Lord that could surmount any obstacle that life puts in front of us. Truly, any success we had, was really God's success. Spontaneous remissions happen all the time. Speak to any long working Oncologist, cancer is beatable. What can be conceived and believed with faith in God can be achieved. The doctor's played a crucial part in Carlette's recovery, however, we believe by faith that God alone healed Carlette. We are blessed. Carlette is now cancer free and a miracle.

Responsibility means taking action. We took several steps and I have listed them below.

1) **See a Doctor.**
   Regular check-ups are vital. If you suspect something is wrong, it is always better to be proactive and have it checked out.

2) **Accept the Assignment**
   If you receive a cancer diagnosis, a part of taking responsibility is praying for the acceptance of the situation, not the cancer.

God never gives us more than we can handle. Carlette also had a schedule of prayer and worship that she lived by. The antidote to fear is faith. I would suggest creating a prayer and worship schedule. Be consistent because it is hard to feel sorry about circumstances when you live with a grateful attitude.

3) **Develop a Hobby or Creative Activity.**
   Keeping your mind focused on things you enjoy will keep your mind free of contaminating thoughts. Carlette also found that writing a gratitude list and thanking God every day for her blessings, aided her in healing. Additionally, go out on dates, learn a new craft like painting, or any other fun activity.

4) **Take Responsibility.**
   Carlette and I took responsibility of the situation. Remember, the actions you take are yours, but the results are God's.

5) **Guard what comes out of your mouth and heart**.
   We were careful to avoid identifying the cancer with Carlette. I will use an example: There is a big difference between someone saying I am depressed, and I have feelings of depression. Feelings come and go. The first example is of someone who says they are depressed or says that they have cancer. When this happens, it means they are internalizing their feelings. And

doing so, it essentially becomes a part of them. Carlette did not look at cancer as being a part of her, but rather as a challenging situation. She worked hard on separating cancer from her identity in Christ. She termed it an alien invader. She also responded to others that she was diagnosed with cancer, never that she had cancer. She knew by faith, with enough pressure it would have no other choice but to leave. Each morning she reaffirmed her health and asked God to deliver her. I know it may sound funny to hear the term "alien invader," but she refused to accept that cancer was part of her body.

6) **Remove negativity.**

Expect people to give you their perspectives. It's human nature to try to diagnose and solve everyone's issues. The opinions of others aren't guaranteed to be formed out of love, wisdom nor discernment. Carlette received several negative comments. Some tried to tie the cancer to smoking, unforgiveness, etc. People will assume that it is your fault or that you have done something to deserve the trial. These comments can push you into a place of deep woundedness, but you must fight to keep your heart pure. No one deserves cancer or any other illness. Separate from all toxic comments and individuals and stay focused on God.

7) **Stay in the present.**

Both of us tried to stay in the present and not give in to our feelings, frustrations, or emotions. We wanted our lives to continue forward and have some normalcy. We stayed present to what was happening in lives besides the cancer. Carlette went on to get her MBA, and I continued working. We took the responsibility to enjoy one another and raise our son Christian. We continuously told cancer to get behind us, just as our Lord said to Satan, "Get thee behind me Satan."

8) **Trust the process**.

At times life's interruptions may throw you for a loop. You may wonder why God has allowed it to happen? Keep your perspectives clear and know that God will never let you go beyond what you can bear. In addition to praying, try to relax and trust the process. Stress and anxiety may contribute to other issues and health maladies. To avoid that, be patient and trust that God knows what He is doing. Trust in His word.

9) **Continue to be open and honest.**

Clear communication is key. Be open and transparent about your feelings. It's okay to take "me" time. Everyone needs space. There may be something that you need to deal with alone. In doing this, never make your partner feel isolated during the process. Clearly communicate your feelings and if you need a crying moment, know that it is okay. Crying can be healthy. Validate your partners feelings, by acknowledging and accepting them. Choose your words wisely so that you are building them up and not tearing them down. If you feel words bubbling up out of an emotional place, take a moment and think before you speak. Remember that communication isn't always verbal. Non-verbal communication is just as important. Find ways to foster and nurture a loving environment. Surprise gifts and little notes around the house can mean lot. And never negate, affection and compliments. Sometimes, it's the little things that mean the most. Remember to keep cancer as the fight, not one another.

10) **Make an effort to understand what your significant other deals with (on all sides).** Knowledge is power. If doing research on your own isn't easy, be sure to be attentive at doctor's visits so that you understand the entire process after the diagnosis. This is going to require a lot of sensitivity and understanding on the part of the supporting spouse or significant other. There is a process toward healing, from the first place of the port, chemo, radiation, surgery, and recovery. Showing compassion and sensitivity regarding the mental and physical changes that your

spouse or significant other will experience will be key in keeping their spirits high and keeping them motivated to continue in the fight. Along with actually enduring the cancer, the diagnosed partner must also be willing to allow their spouse room to deal with all that is taking place. They will need sensitivity and compassion as well. While Carlette and I went through our transition, I battled a lot of emotions. One moment, I'd find myself crying, and the next minute, I was playing superman and trying to save the world. I was secretly praying that she would also understand my heart and emotions.

11) **Love one another.**

Love is the glue that keeps everything flowing. Love kept up motivated. Love kept us sane. Love kept me loving on my wife and her loving on me.

ABOUT THE AUTHORS

Chris and Carlette Edwards have spent over 20 years as pastors. They are true servants, with hearts and the desire to serve God's people in the spirit of excellence and from a kingdom mindset.

Since their genesis in Christ, they were taught how to pray and to walk in faith. Their life and ministry are built around seeing the glory of God manifested in their lives and in the lives of others. They believe God's grace is sufficient for all.

Chris and Carlette are also Marketplace Ministers. For over 10 years, Chris has been the founder & CEO of Edwards Media Group, LLC. He is an ever growing mogul in Christian music, concert and promotional videos. Past clients include legendary singer Shirley Murdock, Lucinda Moore, The Anointed Pace Sisters, Darwin Hobbs, and The Rance Allen Group. Chris directed and produced Dr. Scott's *Be Lifted Up* CD and DVD. They are the authors of *Life's Interruptions-His Beauty, Her Battle.* They host the podcast, *"Live with Chris & Carlette."* The podcast is designed to discuss "life interruptions...the good, bad and the ugly."

Carlette received her prophetic training under the tutelage of Apostle Barbara McClain Ministries; and they both received their ministerial leadership training under Dr. Leonard Scott of Rock Community Church and Dr. Christopher Holland of The Father's House. In addition to Carlette's call to intercessory prayer and the prophetic, she teaches on altar etiquette and church structure. One of her favorite classes to teach is titled, *"I love you, but help me to like you,"* which address the social qualms in the church body.

Chris and Carlette are also inspirational speakers, and they are available to speak at leadership meetings, women's conferences, marriage retreats, altar trainings, and prayer summits. To book the Edwards to speak, please email them at: contact@chrisandcarlette.com.